Wife Material

IDELLA LISELLE

WIFE MATERIAL

This book, or parts thereof, may not be reproduced in any form, stored in a retrieval system, or transmitted in any form by any means—electronic, mechanical, photocopy, recording, or otherwise without prior written permission of the author as provided by the United States of America copyright law.

Scripture quotations taken from the Amplified® Bible,
Copyright © 1954, 1958, 1962, 1964, 1965, 1987 by The Lockman Foundation Used by permission. (**www.Lockman.org**)

Scripture quotations from **THE MESSAGE**. Copyright © by Eugene H. Peterson 1993, 1994, 1995, 1996, 2000, 2001, 2002. Used by permission of NavPress Publishing Group.

Scripture quotations marked "ESV" are taken from The Holy Bible: English Standard Version, copyright 2001, Wheaton: Good News Publishers. Used by permission. All rights reserved.

Scripture quotations marked "KJV" are taken from the Holy Bible, King James Version, Cambridge, 1769.

Scripture quotations taken from the New American Standard Bible® (NASB),
Copyright © 1960, 1962, 1963, 1968, 1971, 1972, 1973, 1975, 1977, 1995 by The
Lockman Foundation Used by permission. www.Lockman.org

Copyright © 2019 All rights reserved
ISBN 13: 9781948731034

Publish*her* Publishing

www.publishher.org

DEDICATION

This is dedicated to every Christian woman married and/or desires to be married who knows that being saved is not enough to save a marriage. As Christians, we were clothed with CHRIST but have we been intentional about being clothed with wife? May this book add material to clothe you as wife and aid in the success of your marriage.

CONTENTS

ACKNOWLEDGEMENTS

Wife Material	9
Who Am I	35
A Dream That Became a Reality	49
Rome Wasn't Built in a Day	61
From Me to We	86
How We Made It Through the Storm	113
Different Requires Different	135
The Darkness Behind the Scenes	146
It's Me, It's Me, It's Me, Oh LORD	164
About the Authors	180

Acknowledgements

To the greatest Author that ever was. The One who wrote my story before the hands of time began and determined that it would be a best seller. He is the one who freely gives inspiration for every book I write, my Mighty Three—GOD, JESUS CHRIST, & HOLY SPIRIT. I and truly, utterly and wholeheartedly love You.

To Wife Material's amazing contributing writers: It was a sublime pleasure working with you. I love the GOD in you and your uncommon transparency. Your stories touched me, so I am confident they are going to touch so many others and help their marriages either before or after they say I do.

Dad, Bonus Mom, Sisters, Brother, Niece and Nephew, I love each of you dearly. Thank you for your support. You allowed me to be me and serve GOD in my purpose so completely and unashamedly despite the fact that it once robbed us of precious moments and memories because of ignorance and imbalance. Thank you for your forgiveness and understanding.

My REAL Ministries Family & Partners, I am honored to be your pastor and truly feel like I am blessed to lead some of the realest, powerful and amazing folks in the world with the biggest hearts for GOD and people. You make leading feel like a treat and privilege on so many levels. It is your support that makes it possible to lend myself to the world and do what I do.

WIFE MATERIAL

1
Wife Material
Idella Liselle

One day as I was praying for marriages, my heart was grieved. Countless wives were hurting and dealing with unnecessary hurdles, traumas, and for some, even divorce. So many women had found themselves in this predicament because they went into marriage unknowingly deaf, dumb, and blind to the true purpose of marriage. The number of wives facing this reality saddened me. So many marriages were being destroyed because of a lack of knowledge. I was consistently receiving cries of frustration about marriage, especially from wives. This pain was exacerbated by the fact that this was happening to Christians. Wasn't CHRIST the fix all and be all? Shouldn't the state of being saved be able to save a marriage? As I snotted and cried, I heard,

"They were clothed with CHRIST, but were they clothed with 'wife?'"

But put on the Lord Jesus Christ, and make no provision for the desires of the flesh...
Romans 13:14 ESV

As He spoke, the above Scripture immediately came to mind. This Scripture is preventative in nature. Putting on CHRIST stops demise and destruction. Is it possible that "putting on wife" would also serve the same purpose? Is this what is missing from many marriages?

Let me interrupt for a moment because I can hear your thoughts. Many are asking, "What about the men?" This by no means lessens the need or responsibility for men to be equipped and prepared for marriage, however, I wasn't called to them right now. I was called to you. You are what is most important to me right now.

Let's take a sidebar. The Sidebar Moments included in this book take place when something I've written sparks another window to share a truth or revelation that will add to your understanding and insight.

SIDEBAR Moments: I love the fact that GOD can use any and everything to teach us. We are called to be disciples, which translates as "students" in some vernaculars. We need to be in a position to be an ever learner. This is key to being an effective wife and a person of excellence.

May I have permission to challenge where that mindset and that kind of question can live? Whenever change is available and one looks at someone else, it is revealing an area where we can stand a little more humility. Humility is always teachable.

I recall a time when correction was coming my way and was even revealed to me in a vision. I immediately thought it was for someone else. That mindset in itself was a cry for help. Humility looks like the cry of the disciples when JESUS CHRIST said that someone would betray Him. They replied, "LORD, is it me?" Self-examination, regardless of what someone else is doing, is a mark of maturity. As a child, when I was getting in trouble, I would want to bring attention to what my other siblings may have done in an attempt to remove the spotlight from myself. Now I understand that if the spotlight is on me, it's because GOD desires to reveal something about me to me so that He can in turn reveal me to others in order to show something about Him.

I could not afford to miss this teachable moment because Humility is definitely connected to wife material.

But there are two sides to every coin. The other side of that thought comes from a pain and a cry: "I am doing all I know to do, but what about him?" When you are doing all you know to do and you feel that there is no accountability or help on the other side, you can undoubtedly find yourself overwhelmed and even defeated at times.

The need for things to be fair becomes a bone of contention and grows seeds of bitterness that will choke the life out of any hopes for redemption. I get it. One thing I have come to understand with much pain and awareness is that marriage isn't always fair. Heck-love isn't fair! I recall asking GOD why I always had to be the first to apologize or the first to try to reconcile. He responded, "Whoever is more surrendered to love in that situation will be the first to react and respond to love's responsibility." Please be encouraged. I truly believe that your present suffering is not worthy to be compared with the glory that will be revealed in you and in your marriage. Don't give up! Let's carry on.

    Scripture reveals the principle that a threefold cord is not easily broken. Marriage is a threefold cord. It is you partnering with the spiritual and the natural. Numerous people put on the spiritual and have forgotten the natural, so daily things that needed to be done on earth were neglected.

I have heard some horror stories of how people would spend hours upon hours in the presence of GOD but refused to give their spouses the same level of interest. There were people who had gone so far as to deny their spouses access to their bedroom for hours, even days, because they were in the presence of GOD with fasting and prayer. That is out of order!

SIDEBAR MOMENT: To all the "deep folk," Scripture advises that when married, fasting requires the permission of a spouse. I am not telling anyone to stop fasting, but I'm advising you to simply be strategic. I know marriage will not stop my fasting lifestyle; however, it will change it. I am able to do uninterrupted long fasts for up to 21 and even 40 days. However, once I get married, I am going to be very mindful of my husband's sex cycle. For those who don't know, each man has a sex cycle. This is the time span that your husband can last without sex and not have an attitude. Pay attention. Some of that frustration you are seeing could simply mean that you need to "put it on him," quick fast, and in a hurry. Fast when your husband is away on trips or at work, and always seek permission to fast for extended times that will affect your sex life.

Back to the story.

But I get it. One of the things that I discovered early on was that church was a great breeding ground for us to become great women of GOD. However, when I started dealing with men on a romantic level, I recognize that I had no confidence in me simply being a woman. I knew how to serve GOD and church and in turn produced amazing fruit, but my interactions with a man didn't yield the same results.

We are told to lead with our strengths, right? In the spirit, I could leap over walls and run over troops. I could slay demons all day and prophecy with accuracy and detail to the masses. I was a powerhouse in the spirit, and the astounding evidence of that was in fact. Yet as a woman in the natural, I didn't have the same backing evidence.

I enter all my relationships under the guise of purpose. So even if they don't end in marriage, they have still served my purpose. A man in one relationship that I was blessed to have once called me out on my deep camouflage. You see, I hid behind my spiritual side because I felt inadequate in my natural side. He too was a pastor, and he challenged me to learn how to be "Idella, the woman."

I would bombard him with prayers and prophecies. I wanted to show off the characteristics that would make me a valuable asset. Spiritually, I knew how to uphold a man. I mean, I was knocking down walls and turning over tables in the spiritual realm on the behalf of men. My prayers were answered in the most amazing ways, but in the beginning, as I was learning myself, I would miss opportunities to be their oasis and safe place.

My spiritual side always wanted to fix things, bring order, and give instructions. My spiritual side and calling had me walking in a role that in the natural wasn't mine to fill. You see, I am a leader, a mover and shaker, and for over a decade, I have grown significantly accustomed to people doing as I say. I had to learn how to take that off and allow the man in the relationship to lead. It was truly a process.

One occasion, I was visiting a friend at his business and wanted to help him. I immediately sprang into action, and he asked me to stop and to just rest.

I was like, "No. You need help, and that is what I am here for." Then he responded, "You simply being here is helping me. Just sit." Sitting down was the most uncomfortable thing in the world. I even began to develop a bad attitude. As I sat, HOLY SPIRIT started ministering to me. He said, "Do you realize what He is saying to you? He is saying that *you* are enough." HOLY SPIRIT continued speaking and shared that I led my relationships with my "do," what I did for a man in service rather than in presence, which was my "be."

It was in that moment that I allowed HOLY SPIRIT to heal the revealed brokenness. In times past, people connected with me for what I could do, especially in ministry, so I had conditioned myself to believe that if I didn't do something, I wouldn't be wanted or needed. I had allowed my insecurities to convince me that my "be" wasn't enough. Listen and please get this. One of the most important things that you need to put on as a wife is the full awareness and acceptance that YOU are enough! Outside of that, you will always be in a place of question and doubt about who you are and who you are to your husband.

Those constant questions cause double-mindedness. This state of mind guarantees that, in regards to your marriage, you will ultimately get nothing that you desire from GOD. It is my prayer that this book will remove your doubt and provide a confidence that will yield an amazing reward in your marriage.

As HOLY SPIRIT continued to share about this wife material principle, this book was launched.

Earlier in ministry, I would be hesitant to speak on issues concerning marriage due to the belief that a single person cannot advise a married person. I bought that lie, line, hook, and sinker. Then one day, HOLY SPIRIT challenged me and asked me if JESUS CHRIST was married. I answered, "no." He asked if Paul was married. Again, I answered, "no." He said, "Well then, did they have wisdom to share about marriages?" I answered, "yes." He then pointed me to the

Scriptures that talk of a wisdom that is pure and unerring, a wisdom that comes from above and how not all wisdom comes through experience. When I coach couples, it is my goal to only say that which I hear and see of the Father, which is governed by the Word. That is the only guarantee one can provide.

Our experiences outside of the Word have no backing power. I don't lead with my experiences. I lead with the Word, and this is why I believe I have been able to have so much success in areas in which I may lack natural experience.

Let me share my journey.

In my early 20s, I was obsessed with getting married. In fact, I actually think it started when I was a little younger than that. Marriage was my destination and my completion. In my daily conversation and contemplation, all roads led to marriage. I can now admit that much of the earlier appeal of marriage was connected to my strong desire to have sex. I wanted to have sex, and for me, marriage was the only option.

I fantasized about marriage, romanticized about marriage. Marriage would connect me with my Prince Charming, my personal rescue. I wholeheartedly bought that famous line from

Jerry McGuire: "You Complete Me." For me, marriage would right all my wrongs and connect me with destiny.

During that time, I connected with a group of young ladies whose end game was marriage as well. Our conversations would all begin and end with "when we get married this, and I can't wait to get married to do that." For a while, this seemed quite normal. Even sermons and messages seemed to promote marriage as a prerequisite to be effective in the Kingdom. Whether directly or indirectly, the message that destiny isn't fulfilled without marriage was being pushed.

This pushed my obsession into overdrive. Every eligible bachelor I met came with the question, "could he be it?" It started to create a neediness in me that was not a good look. This neediness started repelling what I desired and attracted what I did not want. This cycle went uninterrupted for a while.

I continued to believe the fairy tale that marriage would be the fix for my boring life. This attitude caused me to deny the need for responsibility and action in other areas of my life. If marriage was the fix, then something and someone else would have all the responsibility for change.

I was in for a sad awakening. I had very unrealistic expectations about marriage. I originally thought that a good marriage only required both parties to be saved, love the LORD, and love each other. It takes more, a whole lot more. I quickly grew to understand that not all love or commitment is equal, and without a conversation, you can be married to a believer and still be unequally yoked.

Marriage is a complex thing. I previously believed, stated repeatedly, and promoted the idea that "marriage is hard work." This was recently corrected by HOLY SPIRIT. He told me, "It isn't that marriage is hard work. It is that marriage is constant surrender. When people are not willing to surrender and do it my way, it becomes hard work." Wow! Surrender is powerful.

GOD speaks to me plainly through HOLY SPIRIT. These conversations are as constant and clear as If I were conversing with you directly. Back in May of 2007, I heard very clearly that I was getting married on 7/7/7. This information was music to my ears. My faith was on ten. If

GOD said it, then that settled it. I was so convinced that I was looking for invitations. I knew it was going down. During that time, I felt a strong urge to do a 40-day fast. Fasting was a frequent practice for me. I was brought up with fasting being a part of our lifestyle. I had done three, seven, ten, and even 21-day fasts, but I had never done a 40-day fast. My mother had done one, so I shared my desire with her. She was a little concerned because when she fasted, she was able to escape to the mountains, but I would still be working full time in ministry as the Youth Director during this fast. She knew that my hours were demanding, and so were my responsibilities. I listened to her concerns but still felt that I was being led to fast, and the desire would not go away.

I started the fast which literally changed my life. As I was nearing the end, I was forwarded a prophetic message from a well-known prophet. It was sent to me because what I had been sharing and hearing in the spirit was very similar, if not identical, to what GOD was speaking to the prophet. As I read it, I was in awe of the confirmation I saw regarding certain spiritual matters. I wasn't ready for what I read at the end of the article. It mentioned that the prophet had been charged to do a 40-day fast that would end on 7/7/7. The last day was to be the wedding. The body of CHRIST needed to enter into a greater covenant with CHRIST. I smiled and chuckled. This was the wedding HOLY SPIRIT was referring to. Thank GOD, I didn't send any invitations.

GOD shared with me that I was ready to *get* married but wasn't ready to *be* married. This again refers to the process to simply be. He told me that if I submitted and surrendered to Him, He would teach me how to be a wife. As I became a good wife to Him, I would be a great wife to my husband when he came along. Over the years, I have been sitting at His feet like Mary, gaining things that can't be robbed from me, and studying marriage. Praying about and for marriages has also provided preparation.

Many people end in divorce because they were ready to get married but not ready to be married. "Be" is a whole other playing field.

Let's define "Be"

First, I want to ensure that you know the "be" of any marriage will deal with the past and present and determine your future. Marriage draws on all of your experiences. This is why it is imperative to come into marriage whole, as whole as you possibly can be. I believe one of the designs of marriage is to challenge who you are and pull out of you things only your spouse can do. That level of intimacy serves as a buffeter. Gary Chapman made a statement in his book, *Sacred Marriage*, that continues to stay with me: "What if marriage was created to make us holy more than happy?" It puts things in perspective.

GOD created marriage to serve as a tool for our greatness and cultivation. Often, we forfeit the benefits of marriage because we have yet to connect with its purpose.

Let us go further with the "be" or purpose of marriage.

Definition of "be": to equal in meaning; have the same connotation as; SYMBOLIZE
Ex: GOD is Love.

Our marriages should be equal in meaning to the covenant JESUS CHRIST made with the church. The body is referred to as the bride and CHRIST the husband. We have to walk in unconditional love with our spouses. I recall one of my relationships that GOD truly used to teach and train me. I had shared with my boyfriend something that GOD had shared with me. He was my biggest supporter. Whenever I did anything, if he was able to be there, he was there. He was my go-to person. On one occasion, his hesitancy to back what I said gave me an attitude because I took it personally. Under my pressure, he acquiesced, but I was still feeling some kind of way. When he called back later that day, I didn't answer because I didn't feel like talking. HOLY SPIRIT immediately chastised me with the question, "Oh, so that is what your love looks like? It is conditional. You only love when people do what you want them to do." I was crushed. I thought I was so loving and caring, but that moment revealed an ugliness that needed immediate correction. I later called him and repented.

Magnify that encounter by 10,000, and that is the level of cultivation that comes with marriage. Marriage doesn't allow you to get away from the challenge. It is in your face 24/7, and if you aren't looking at it through the lens of love described in 1 Corinthians 13, you are definitely going to have a problem.

SIDEBAR MOMENT: Is Your Love conditional? Many of us don't have a full understanding of kingdom-style love. Our love is temporal and therefore very temporary. The longevity of our love and relationships is conditional. If others don't do what we want them to do or respond how we want them to respond, we start treating them differently. I am convinced that many of US don't really know how to love like GOD. GOD's love is agape love. It comes from the mind, not the heart, and it operates as a choice, not a feeling. Feelings are like the wind. Often, you can't see them coming, but you can feel their effects. I am often in awe of how JESUS CHRIST was able to operate in His relationships. His love truly covered a multitude of sins. He knew both Judas and Peter were going to betray Him and still loved them the same. Man, this is one I have to constantly work on. When I have been betrayed or hurt, I tend to distance myself to protect myself and often fail to deal with the hurt, but that isn't maturity.

In a healthy relationship, it is imperative that you deal with it. Even as I am writing this, HOLY SPIRIT is instructing me to address passive aggressive behavior. I recall when I was hurt by my pastor. I had reached out for help, and my pastor's availability didn't match my need. When we reconnected, I had already resolved the situation but was making veiled comments about how I was able to get it done MYSELF with an attitude behind it. As I hung up, HOLY SPIRIT exposed my passive aggressive behavior, and passive aggression is connected to deception. It covers and hides. Operating under passive aggressive tendencies never directly deals with the issue. It's found in the undertones when someone asks you how you're doing and you respond, "Fine," with an attitude in your voice, knowing full well that you are not fine.

When HOLY SPIRIT brought that to my attention, I called my pastor back and shared how I was hurt by the lack of availability towards me during my time of need. My pastor apologized and explained what was going on. My pastor let me know that, going forward, if the situation was urgent, I should communicate that and in turn receive a response as soon as possible.

Agape love chooses to push through the

minutiae, to focus on the purpose of us being together, to fight (with one another rather than against each other), and to forgive.

Definition of "be:" to have identity with; to constitute the same idea or object as
Ex: My husband and I are one.

In order for marriage to work according to creation, you must be willing to become one with your spouse. This does not deny your individuality. On the contrary, it merges who you are with who he is in order to create and greater representation and advancement for kingdom. Who I am doesn't end or stop when I get married. Instead, it simply becomes greater and more powerful as it connects with my husband's purpose and call. This is the part where I must insert the importance of being equally yoked. Many people have limited that to mean Christians should not marry unbelievers. However, I want to challenge that thought in order to provide a more complete understanding.

The yoke defined in that Scripture refers to the yokes that were placed on the oxen that plowed a field. The oxen were placed side by side and were connected to plow the field. When that yoke wasn't equal, for example, the oxen pulled in different directions, it would cause irritation.

Simply being saved doesn't mean we automatically have the same field of purpose or the same level of pursuit. I know who I am and what I am called to do. It would be foolish to connect with someone whose direction is totally contrary to mine. I am my husband's complement and vice versa.

Another disclaimer is needed. Your husband's salvation doesn't have to be identical to yours. One frustration I often see in powerful women of GOD is that they demand their spouse's relationship to look EXACTLY like their own.

We are told to work out our OWN salvation with fear and trembling. The work of your husband's salvation may look different. For example, you may be one who prays very loudly. Maybe you are very expressive and demonstrative in your worship. Demanding that your husband's prayers and worship be the same is a form of bondage.

The commonality has to be our level of love and obedience. One may be called to platform ministry and another to marketplace ministry. Therefore, the look and work of ministry would be different. My husband doesn't have to hold a mic to minister. For me, that isn't even impressive any longer. I long for someone who lives ministry and does not just preach it. I require a lifestyle of ministry so that at any moment or any time, GOD can use us to bring Him glory.

Check his motive, not his method. Methods can hide motives, so make sure you are looking at the right thing.

I love historical dramas. One thing I saw repeatedly was that kings only gave their children in marriage to people who could advance the kingdom. They opposed allowing marriages that were not beneficial to the kingdom. I have a kingdom outlook on marriage. I truly believe that my marriage was created to do more for the kingdom than I could for myself, and it was created for me to have fun throughout the process.

Let's get back to "be."

Definition of "be": to have an objective existence; have reality or actuality; LIVE
Ex: "I think, therefore I am."

Your marriage is the sum of your thoughts. The way you think about marriage determines what you are willing to do for it. If you see it as drudgery, you will be hesitant to fully invest yourself in it. That mode of thinking will rob you of your joy, which depletes you of your strength. If you see marriage as a gift to be treasured, the way you handle it will be healthy and positive.

Marriage is a privilege. Through it, we get to walk out GOD's love for us towards another person in the most intimate manner.

I love that the word "live" is connected to "be!" What kind of life does your marriage have? Are you bored with your marriage? I recall being a youth and telling my mother that I was bored. Her response was, "Only boring people are bored." She challenged me to use whatever resources I had available to meet my needs in a healthy manner. Her response placed the responsibility on me to cultivate myself. What can you do about yourself to make your marriage better?

I have coached countless couples, and it's interesting when they start talking about their issues how some like to place blame on the other party. Arguments fly out of control when one's aim is to be right over being reconciled.

When you want to be right, you will revel in how the other party is wrong. Reconciliation requires one to look for ways to overcome the offense and move on to fulfill the purpose of one's union. I will share one of my strategies I coach my clients on in regard to relational conflict.

Three R's to Reconciliation
Ask yourself these three things:

Role: What is my role in this? How did I add to the situation? Was there an emotion in me that was operating against the purpose of reconciliation? Did I overlook a way of escape that GOD provided in order for me to avoid the negative outcome?

Responsibility: Change comes with responsibility. What is **MY** responsibility to reconcile? Did I fulfill my responsibility to love my spouse as stated in 1 Corinthians 13?

Repentance: Repentance leads to transformation. When one repents, the situation or circumstance can no longer be the same. Think about some practical ways you can prevent the issue from happening again. When you repent to your spouse, include those practical ways in your presentation of your repentance, and even consider some ways to prevent the issue together. The word says to bring "fruits of repentance" Repentance without fruit can weary a partner and provide an opening for the enemy.

to have, maintain, or occupy a place, situation, or position
Ex: My marriage is in GOD's hands.

Your marriage must be able to maintain its rightful position. That is in the hands of the Father. The reality is, unless GOD builds the house, all your labor is in vain. Keeping your marriage in GOD's hands allows your hands to build your house and not destroy it.

Last, but definitely not least, which is actually my favorite part of "be" is presented in the following:

Definition of be: to remain unmolested, undisturbed, or uninterrupted

When marriage is in the hands of the Father, positioned through obedience and surrender, what the enemy may throw at it ultimately won't trip you up or cause you to lose out. The "be" of your marriage must be healthy and must be maintained in order for its purpose to be fulfilled.

POINTS TO PONDER
1. Are you in your "be"?
2. Your "be" determines your "do."
3. Marriage takes more than just being saved.
4. What natural things have you neglected in your marriage?
5. What spiritual things have you neglected in your marriage?
6. Is Your Love Conditional?

POINTS TO PRACTICE
1. In the face of conflict, before you look out at the other person, make sure that you look inward at yourself.

2. Put things in place to treasure your marriage as a gift.
3. Be in a place of constant development because you are the only one you can change. Your change is able to produce change.

POINTS TO PRAY
FATHER,

We come to You with a "thank You." You are so amazing, and in whatever place we find ourselves, we can rest in the confidence that You are working ALL things out for our good. We repent of our ignorance to any purpose or plan that You have for our marriage. We ask that You would fully reveal Your plan for our marriage and how You desire to use it to advance Your kingdom. We fully align through surrender.

We ask for the mind of CHRIST, which changes our perception and reception. We thank You for the transformation that we get in and through Your Word. We thank You that our marriage is a gift that we will treasure and honor in the natural and in the spiritual. We thank You that we will walk in a greater level of "be" and live our best life yet. In JESUS CHRIST's name we pray, amen!

2
Who Am I?
Debbie Jones

Often, we seek to be loved unconditionally by our spouses when in fact, we first need to learn how to truly love ourselves. I have learned from experience that if you do not know who you are, you will not know how to truly love yourself. If you do not know how to love yourself, it is impossible to know how to truly love someone else, especially your spouse.

My search for true self love uncovered my struggles with personal and family identity. Those struggles were found in my need to please everyone around me, including my husband, and they were found in the inability to speak my truth out loud. The impact of these inward battles that I faced were negatively affecting my marriage. I had clothed myself with my wounds and confusion.

It was time to change for real. I had to try something new. I had to take off fear, rejection, and anxiety. In other words, I had to take off my dysfunction. For me to be a more effective wife, I had to put on true self love, acceptance of myself and others, and peace.

My lack of knowing who I was as a person impacted the way I showed true love to myself and my husband. My personal and family issues with identity had begun long before I got married. However, I was completely unaware that I even had an issue with myself and past experiences. This was brought to my attention at a prayer conference that I attended two years ago. I was told that the rejection that I experienced from my father as a child was one of the root causes of my internal struggle with identity. I realized that this identity thief had been following me all of my life and stealing bits and pieces of me, causing self-doubt and robbing me of being my true self. This affected every relationship, most importantly, my marriage.

Let me share a little family history with you so that you get a better understanding of what I am talking about regarding family identity issues. I was born in Kingston, Jamaica. At the age of three, I immigrated to the United States of America with both my parents along with two siblings. Not long after arriving in this country, my father abandoned our family. As a result, I grew up knowing very little to nothing about my homeland and the many family members that I left behind. This created a longing that was unknown for years.

I married my husband at a very young age. Looking back over my life, I truly believe in my heart that I got married young to fill the void of my father being absent from my life. Do not get me wrong, I married a great man, and he is an even better husband. However, I believe my need for a father played into some of my choices in the past.

In the beginning years of our 25-year marriage, I had put on the identity of a wife chosen by my husband, which means I became who he said I was. During the early years of my marriage, I did not know how to express my feelings about my unseen identity problem to my spouse. I just kept everything that I was feeling and thinking to myself. Having no real sense of self at that time in my life created unresolved issues that were never really addressed until now.

In past years, I did not know that the love I was in need of from my spouse first began with me knowing how to love myself. Recently, I began to take the much-needed steps to improve my self-image and connect to my family heritage.

For me, knowing who I was connected to knowing where I came from. This was needed both in the spiritual and the natural. After receiving that unforgettable revelation and applying what I have been learning about myself from God, my relationship with myself got better. That was a significant reality, and it affected all my other relationships. I saw improvements with my mom, something I had prayed for, my relationship with my husband got better, and our marriage got better too.

People pleasing was something that I did more than I would like to admit. Because of the rejection from my father, I tried in many ways to please my husband in order to gain his acceptance. My emotional state could not handle the idea of being rejected by my husband too. People pleasing was also a strategy that I used to often avoid conflict in my marriage. The thought of my spouse being upset with me brought great anxiety. For example, if my husband said, "I do not like a loud woman." I would internalize that comment and resort to being quiet, hoping that he was not referring to me as the loud woman.

Thank you, God, for delivering me from the need to please others and for teaching me how to say no and be okay with it. Today, I have evolved as a woman and a wife, so those old ways that I used to practice have all passed away. In stark contrast to people pleasing, I now seek to please my Heavenly Father in all things.

I also realized that I had not been speaking my truth out loud. For example, sometimes I said all the things I thought my spouse wanted to hear instead of sharing what was actually on my mind. I was more concerned about being liked and what other people's opinion was of me instead of being heard or voicing my own opinion.

I allowed situations that I was going through to silence me. During difficult times in my life, I did not share my pain with anyone, not even my husband. Our lack of communication created a distance between me and my husband for a time because neither of us knew what to say to each other. Lack of communication was always one of the biggest issues we faced in our marriage overall. This brought on some lonely days and lonely nights at home together. The fact that I can share it now with countless people reading this book shows how far God has brought me in my ability to communicate.

I believe that marriage is based on truth. We have grown closer as a couple since we have learned how to talk things over. Since I started speaking my truth out loud, I have not stopped speaking. Even greater is the fact that God gave me the courage to speak my truth in this book to help other women who may feel like I did, as if their voice has been silenced.

I spent years searching here and there for true love from man when God's love was there all the time, waiting to be unveiled like a bride on her wedding day. Whether we know it or not, God is always with us, and Matthew 28:20 reminds us of this truth as it says, "teaching them to observe all things whatsoever I have commanded you: and, I am with you always even unto the end of the world." God's love gave me the courage to connect with myself in ways that I had never considered before because I knew that I would never have to do things alone.

My God told me in Genesis that I was created in his image:

So God created man in his own image, in the image of God created he him; male and female created he them.
Genesis 1:27 KJV

That statement was powerful for me. It gave me strength to deal with my image problems.

God also reveals this truth in Psalm 139:

I will praise thee for I am fearfully and wonderfully made: marvelous are thy works; and that my soul knoweth right well.
Psalm 139:14 KJV

In Jeremiah, He tells me that his love for me will never end:

The Lord hath appeared of old unto me, saying, Yea, I have loved thee with an everlasting love: therefore, with loving kindness have I drawn thee.

Jeremiah 31:3 KJV

These Scriptures ministered greatly to me in my time of need. God's love helped me find my identity and taught me how to truly love my self and others around me, especially my husband.

Now that I know who I am in Christ, my whole perspective of who I am as a wife has changed dramatically. I have taken off the layers of fear, rejection, and anxiety that wrapped itself around every fiber of my being and enveloped my soul. The garment of fear that I wore daily robbed me of the ability to hear and speak my truth. God is so amazing at the what and how. The idea of this book found me during a period in which I was spending time with my Heavenly Father, discovering what He says about me so that I can reiterate it to myself and truly BE who He says that I am.

No longer am I letting the words of others be sewn deep into my heart like a symbol of their love for me. I wear my new garments of true love, acceptance, and peace that my Heavenly

Father has so tenderly placed on me. God's words of wisdom and true love are masterfully woven into my heart as I daily seek His counsel on how to be my true self and a wife. I am one example of how God can clothe women with wife material.

When I changed for the better on the inside, everything around me began to change for the better too. I am happy to declare that in the last three years; I have reconnected with my dad after decades of not knowing where he was. Last year, my father also introduced me to one of my brothers that I had never met before. Someday soon, I also believe that God will unite me with my two long-lost sisters by faith. So, as you can see, God is restoring my identity. He is restoring my marriage and my family, one stitch at a time. I will rejoice in the Lord for all His wonderful blessings.

I will greatly rejoice in the Lord, my soul shall be joyful in my God; for he hath clothed me with the garments of salvation, he hath covered me with the robe of righteousness, as a bridegroom decketh himself with ornaments, and as a bride adorneth herself with her jewels.

Isaiah 61:10 KJV

In conclusion, my sincere hope is to influence people to think differently about marriage as well as provide you with practical steps to consider in purposefully loving your spouse as you love yourself.

POINTS TO PONDER

Based on my experience, I believe that marriage should never be done in isolation. Every married couple needs a support system or a community of like-minded people with whom they can partner and share life experiences. There are so many marriage-related resources available online as well. Keeping things from coming apart at the seams in a marriage requires a lot of effort, but in the end, it pays off in the form of a healthy marriage.

As you read my story, I challenge you to examine yourself and where you are as a wife. What did you have to remove from your life in order to be a wife, and what did you have to apply in order to be a wife? Have a conversation with God about what wife materials you need in order to be a more effective wife. Although your story or circumstance may be different from mine, we share a common goal of working on being the best wife we can possibly be.

I encourage everyone who is reading these words to spend as much time as possible with God each day. Spending time with God is a simple yet profound exercise that anyone can do. He is never too busy to meet every single one of your needs. He is always available, day or night, early or late, no matter the weather, rain, or shine. Trust me when I tell you that time with Him will be time well spent. I promise that you will not regret it. Just do it! I did. You will reap the benefits for years to come, even for a lifetime. Consistent time with God will transform your life. It transformed mine.

How we view marriage depends on who you are talking to. Our modern-day society's standard for marriage is different from God's Bible-based standard for marriage. According to Scripture, marriage is a covenant created by God, not man.

In Mark 10:6-9, it states: "But from the beginning of the creation God made them male and female. For thus cause shall a man leave his father and mother, and cleave to his wife. And they Twain shall be one flesh. So, then they are no more Twain, but one flesh. What therefore God hath joined together, let not man put asunder." Thus, this Scripture verse clearly states that God joins a man and woman together in marriage, not man.

I wanted to leave you with these points to think about as you continue on your wife-making journey, tying up any loose ends you find along the way in marriage.

POINTS TO PRACTICE

As I was thinking of ideas to write for this particular section, I heard God say, "Do not tell the women what they need to do. Tell them what you did and how I made it work together for your good."

The following activities are practical steps that I incorporated in my marriage to keep it tightly woven together so that things did not fall apart.

- We studied Scriptures on marriage and true love, such as I Corinthians 13:4, "Charity suffereth long, and is kind; charity envieth not; charity vaunteth not itself, is not puffed up."
- I created a vision board describing marriage and family goals for the future. Miraculously, God has made everything I envisioned in my mind and put on the vision board a reality! Amazing God!
- Each day, I would attempt to spend seven minutes of focused time with God. I called it "seven minutes to spare." I chose the number seven because it is the number of completion. Some days, I did more than seven minutes, but a minimum of seven minutes was always the goal. My precious time with the Lord consisted of me reading one or two verses from the Bible and praying or talking to God. Sometimes, I

would go for a walk and just listen to Him speak to me. I would also listen to worship music or music that inspired me to rise above obstacles in my life and move forward. No two days were ever the same, and if I missed a day, then I just tried again the next day. The Bible verses began to come alive in my life, and prayers started shifting my life towards a positive direction. This was a gradual process that happened over time. "Seven minutes to spare" is not an easy challenge, but it is one well worth doing. It brought tremendous healing to my heart, soul, and mind. Trust me, every distraction will come and attempt to steal your time with God, but just keep pressing forward.

- My husband and I attended small-group marriage classes at our church that were called "Married Life." The small group offered couple-centered activities, such as a date night at the movies with a free babysitter included.
- We read books on marriage and love, such as *The 5 Love Languages* by Gary Chapman.
- We attended a marriage conference that was called "The Marriage I Have Always Wanted."

- We connected with a couple (we called them our covenant couple) that we knew and trusted to mentor us and we them. We discussed marriage-related topics in person over a meal or via telephone conversations

POINTS TO PRAY

In 1 Thessalonians 5:17, the word of God charges us to "pray without ceasing." Thus, I did not give up praying when I did not see changes right away in my marriage. I participated in a powerful prayer line called The Remnant Call by REAL Ministries. That increased my knowledge of prayer and led to me praying out loud for others at church and beyond. In addition, I attended an unforgettable prayer conference that provided me with more instruction on prayer.

Prayer was the saving grace in my marriage that helped me grow closer to God and to my spouse. I believe that prayer is simply opening your mouth and talking to God. Prayer is also being still and listening to what God has to say to you. There were many times in my marriage when I found myself in a situation where I did not know what to do, so I began to pray. Like my mom always said to me, "prayer works." She was so right! As I began to see the real changes that prayer was making in my life, I began to pray more. Sometimes, I did not know what words to pray, so I began to search through Scripture. I prayed directly from the Word of God. A friend told me that when people pray the Word of God, they are speaking the language of God. I would look up one word in the Bible concordance, such as "peace," and I would pray those verses on peace that spoke to whatever situation I was going through at the time. Through continuous prayer, I surrendered fear, rejection, and anxiety to God. In exchange, God adorned me with His true love, acceptance, and peace.

When faced with trials and tribulations in my marriage, I stood on words from Mathew 22 for strength:

Master, which is the great commandment in the law? Jesus said unto him, Thou shalt love the Lord thy God with all thy heart, and with all thy soul, and with all thy mind. This is the first and great commandment.... Thou shalt love thy neighbor as thyself.   *Matthew 22:36-39 KJV*

I believe if I get a greater understanding of this Scripture and apply it to every area of my life, especially marriage, everything else will begin to fall in place for me. The Bible verse found in Matthew 22:36-39 emphasizes true love for God, self, and others as the key to everyday success.

Lord, teach me how to truly love You with all my heart, all my soul, and all my mind. Teach me how to truly love myself and others, in Jesus' name. Amen.

3

A Dream That Became a Reality
Myrlene Warren

I have always heard people talk about getting married or having a fantasy wedding. I was one of them. I wanted to have a beautiful wedding that was over the top, and I did! I can remember the moment on the day of my wedding when my Pastor introduced my husband and me as husband and wife. It was the greatest feeling in the world. I felt so amazing. I had so many different thoughts going through my head. I remember thinking, "Wow! I am a wife now. I can't believe I am married!" It was like a dream come true. All these excitements were great, but just being married or having a beautiful wedding doesn't define a great wife or marriage. After the celebration is over and everyone is gone, knowing that my dream had become a reality and wondering what was next, I now had to figure out how to start my journey.

I was never taught what it would take to be a wife, nor was I taught what marriage would be like. My perception of marriage was fantasy-based. I envisioned waking up to my husband and enjoying him, which I did! In addition, I would spend a lot of time thinking about what we'd do on a regular basis—the different activities we would do together inside and outside of our home and the career and life goals we would accomplish together. But I never considered the work it required or what tools I was going to need in order for me to be an effective wife. As a result, I found myself free styling. That is operating with no sense of direction. I was doing things I thought I should do based on my own observations.

Secret Expectations

Coming into marriage not knowing much, I had a list of expectations—expectations of what marriage should look and be like. I believed that a happy wife would automatically result in a great marriage. With this perspective in mind, my list included things my husband should do to satisfy me. Everything would cater to my own wants and needs, nothing for my husband. I eventually realized that I had a high expectation of what I wanted from my husband, but I did not consider what I needed to be a good wife for my husband.

Not only did I have a list of expectations, but I failed to communicate them to my husband. It was basically a list of secret expectations as I simply assumed that my spouse already knew what they were. In a way, I acted as though I expected my husband to be a mind reader. In addition, I blamed him when my expectations were not met. If he did not operate the way I wanted, then it was a problem. I can remember having a bad attitude or using harsh words just because things were not going as I expected.

While reading the Word, I came across this Scripture:

A gentle answer quiets anger, but a harsh one stirs it up. When wise people speak, they make knowledge attractive, but stupid people spouse nonsense.

Proverbs 15:1-2 GNT

After reading this, I had to pray and ask God to help me to do better. When I evaluated myself and the way things were going in my marriage, I learned that placing all of the responsibility on my partner created confusion in our marriage and was not healthy. I remember the days in which my husband was trying to figure out what was wrong with me based on my emotions or behavior, but he could not. I would shut down and not say anything. Later, I would bring up whatever issue was related to why I was displeased.

I realized that my Husband did not want me to remain silent and assume that he already knew what I was feeling and why. After I would make that assumption, he would usually pose the same question, "Why didn't you say something?" And when I did speak up, he would always make sure the situation was addressed. As a result, I quickly learned that I needed to replace secret expectations with effective communication if I wanted my marriage to work.

Communication has always been important to me. I always used to say that I wanted a mate who would listen, pay attention, and interact with me. Nevertheless, I found out that there is more to these characteristics in a marriage. You must know the right way to translate the information without offending your partner. It took me a while to learn that it is not only what you say that is important, but how you say it carries a lot of weight. I continuously used to find ways to criticize the situation when it did not work out to my favor. I remembered getting mad at my Husband one day because I wanted to spend time with him, but he was playing a game on his phone. I recalled saying something slick to him. He then stated that all I had to say was, "Let's go do something." Immediately, he said, "Baby, let's go outside and take a walk." As I walked outside with him smiling, I thought about how the way our words come out really matter.

One Size Doesn't Fit All

Categorizing my spouse was one of the few things I did in my marriage. In other words, I judged him and/or put him into categories based on observations. Growing up, I did not experience a healthy marriage. I had to search for places and people from mass media, social media, or unknown strangers to determine what a good marriage looked like. With that, I studied what I saw amongst couples in the outside world. I observed all the cute pictures that couples would take/post together, the nice vacations they would take, the nice posts they put out on social media, etc. I saw all of those things as a sign of a good marriage. Such beliefs affected the relationship I had with my mate. I expected my spouse to act based on skewed, preconceived notions. I then held him accountable for the standards he failed to meet.

After a while of behaving that way, I learned that I did not know my husband for who he was. I had been trying to make him someone that he was not. As I focused on the stranger, I was never satisfied, even when my man was doing the best, he could do for me. I battled with this for a couple of years early on in my marriage.

I eventually reached a turning point when I found out the same couples I tried to emulate did not last. The same couples who were broadcasting the nice pictures and posts were the same people who cheated or even abused their spouses. These types of situations helped me to gain insight that I had to stop comparing my husband and see him for who he was.

See Your Spouse For Who He Is

When I started seeing my husband for who he was, I discovered that everything I wanted in a guy was right here in front of me, my husband. I started to see and appreciate all the little things my spouse was doing for me. He always focused on my well-being. On various occasions, I would ask my husband what he wanted, he would turn it around and ask me the same question. At first, I used to get very frustrated. It took me awhile to see he was really making it about me. He was basically saying that if I wanted it, then he was satisfied to comply. However, because I was so focused on the way the outside world was doing things, I could not see how privileged I was to have a husband that catered to my needs.

As I paid more attention, I was able to see the great husband that I was not able to see before and how grateful I was to be his wife. When I paid attention, I noticed he would always speak so well of me. When my husband would speak of his wife, he would say things as though I was the most perfect wife in the world. I realized that although I was not perfect, he was not keeping a list of what I did wrong. Instead, he was keeping a list of what I did right. I was reminded of what love really is, especially after reading 1 Corinthians 13:

Love is patient, love is kind. It does not envy, it does not boast, it is not proud. It does not dishonor others, it is not self-seeking, it is not easily angered, it keeps no record of wrongs
1 Corinthians 13:4-5 NIV

The part that stood out the most for me states that love "keeps no record of wrongs." That was confirmation and conviction for change. This became my real model of love.

Conflicts vs. Solution

When conflicts or disagreements come, how do you handle them? At the beginning of our marriage, nagging was how I dealt with conflicts. I mean, I really fussed about everything, even the smallest things. Putting things in the right place was a significant priority for me. I was raised in a home that was very neat, and I was required to clean daily and have everything in the right order. When I moved in with my mate, I carried the same routine. If my husband removed his clothes and did not put it where it belonged, I would get upset and run my mouth. This behavior became an issue in my marriage. However, at that time, I did not know that.

One day, as I was talking on the phone with my Mother in-law, Tracey Baker, she asked, "How is it going with you guys?" I answered, "We are doing fine, but I'm just frustrated with how my husband doesn't clean up after himself and leaves things everywhere." She took me straight to the bible. She quoted Proverbs 114:1, NLT: "A wise woman builds her home, but a foolish woman tears it down with her own hands." This was all I needed to hear. My whole mindset changed forever because I did not want to be a foolish woman who would destroy my home. With that in mind, it was important for me to know my position in my marriage. By praying and seeking knowledge and wisdom, I was reminded to focus on solutions rather than problems. I had to change my mindset from focusing on what was not working to focusing on what was working. I challenged myself to bring out the good in every situation instead of the bad.

Nagging was one of the problems that I had to create a solution for. Nagging may have different meanings for different individuals. For me, nagging is to continuously complain about a situation or something that I want to change. However, what I found out is nagging does not make a man move. The more I used to complain and force my husband to move, the more reluctant he became. Instead of fussing at my husband for placing his clothes in the wrong place, I got a basket and placed it in the area where he usually puts his items, which made it easier and convenient. So, instead of putting his belongings on the floor or out of place, he would put it in the basket most of the time. In addition, if my home was not clean to the standards, I would want it to be and I didn't have time to do it myself, I would not nag my husband. Instead, I would usually say something like this, "Boo, can you clean up for me, please?" He usually amazed me and would exceed my expectations. Also, I tried to replace nagging with acknowledgment and appreciation. Instead of bringing up the negative in a situation, I would acknowledge the positive and thank him for it. This really works. When I do this, I can see in his eyes that he feels appreciated.

Our Differences Matter

My husband and I come from a totally different cultural background. I am Haitian American, born in Haiti. I came to the U.S. when I was 12 years old. My husband is African American, born in a small country town called Pahokee, Florida. With us being from different backgrounds, we are very different. He was taught things one way from his home or culture, and I was taught things another way. So, it was a conflict for us when his methods did not match mine. When our beliefs clashed, it translated into actions. I would proceed however I wanted to because I believed that my way was how it should be done, and he would do things his way. This really caused a major problem in our marriage. I knew then that we couldn't continue to operate that way if we were going to make our marriage work. It was then my husband and I decided we needed to create our own culture for our marriage, home, and family. This required us to combine our ideas and efforts and resulted in much success.

POINTS TO PONDER

Do not compare your marriage with others. Every household is different, and one never knows how a person's marriage is going based on appearance. If you focus on comparing your spouse with others, you will never get to know who your partner really is. Furthermore, in doing so, you will never get to a place where you can appreciate your spouse.

How do you handle conflicts? A beautiful marriage is not one that does not have conflicts. In fact, I believe great marriages will experience disagreements, hardships, and difficulties. However, when the hard times come, the way you handle them will make a difference. Knowing what to do or who to call when troubles come is very important.

A person's cultural norms and values are always very important. However, make sure you don't get so stuck to your own way of doing things and allow that to drive your marriage. Keep in mind that your beliefs may be different from those of your spouse. The best thing to do is to come into agreement or create your own culture for your marriage with your spouse.

POINTS TO PRACTICE

It is very simple to make a list of what our spouses are not doing. Instead of keeping a list of wrongs, make a list of the things your spouse is doing right. I have done this in my own marriage. What I realized was the good characteristics outweigh the petty issues. When I wanted to fuss about nonsense, I was quickly reminded of the "good list," which calmed me down.

Couples need to set a strong foundation for their marriage. When the hard times come, knowing the right resources to use is very important. For my spouse and me, going to the Word and praying has become our source for resolving issues. We allow God to be the blueprint of our marriage. As a couple, we seek God for help, direction, and clarity because we understand that we are not able to get through anything without Him. Some couples may call on a friend, parent, or church leaders during difficulties in their marriage. There is nothing wrong with calling on these people, but make sure they are trustworthy. Don't call on people who are going to give you bad advice or tear your marriage apart.

It is very easy to focus on problems in a marriage. This happens unintentionally because life comes with difficulties and hardships. Allowing problems to drive your marriage may cause your marriage to fail because problems will make you feel stuck. Instead, focus on solutions rather than problems. What solution gives you hope? This lets you know there is a way out and things can change for the better. When issues come up, ask God to show you the positive side of the situation, and have hope that it will change. Pray continuously as prayer changes things.

POINTS TO PRAY

Father, we thank you for our marriage. Thank you for allowing us the opportunity to be in this union with one another. We pray that You continue to bless this union and show us favor. Thank You, Father, for giving us Your words to rely on during times of difficulty. Thank you for

clarity and wisdom in our marriage. We are going to stand on Your words according to Mark 10:9: "Let no one split apart what God has joined together." Father God, despite all of the struggles we face, we will not allow anything to break us apart. We are claiming a strong lifetime marriage, in Jesus' name. Amen!

4
Rome Wasn't Built in a Day (Neither is Marriage)
Orienthia Speakman

Rome had been on my bucket list ever since I could remember. As a little girl, I was always fascinated by its culture and fashion. But to be quite honest, it was the stories of the battles that took place in the Colosseum that really sparked my curiosity. My father had this same fascination with Rome and the Gladiators that he taught me his version of the stories he had read. We even watched *Ben-Hur* together over and over again because it was a story of a Jewish nobleman during the time of Jesus Christ, a story of a man who was turned into a slave by the Romans. This slave won his freedom and came back for revenge. *Ben-Hur* fought in the Colosseum, and that visual, although it may not be a true story, stuck in my mind. All of this added to my fantasy of one day walking those grounds.

Rome, the capital of Italy and considered the capital of the ancient empire, is a place where The Vatican, The Pantheon, and even The Colosseum reside. Rome is a city that has been credited for producing big labels, such as Gucci, Dolce and Gabbana, Versace, and even Prada. It is a landmark that is popular for some of the most traditional Italian cuisine, which includes spaghetti, pasta Carbonara, risotto, lasagna, and even pizza!

Rome is such a landmark that in 2018, more than 7.4 million tourists traveled to partake in all that it could offer. It is considered the most popular tourist attraction in the world, and that is not likely to change anytime soon. My husband and I were a couple out of those 7.4 million tourists as we had an opportunity to visit for our eighth wedding anniversary.

As tourists in Rome, we had a strategy laid out to see all the so-called hottest spots there. My husband, Vincent, and I originally decided that we would self-tour the city. Keep in mind that we were in a foreign country, we had no family or friends there, Italian is not a language that either one of us speak fluently, and besides all of that, we hadn't asked for help from anyone that may be familiar with the process of how these tours worked. We had planned it all out in our minds how great this week would be without considering any roadblocks or barriers we might encounter.

Most of us enter our marriages the same way, let alone how we enter our role as a wife. We either observe someone else's marriage and think, "Oh, this will be easy," or we have a preconceived notion that we know it won't be all sunny skies without seriously considering all the barriers that we could possibly face.

I find myself often saying in women's conferences, "Being a wife is one of the most fulfilling and frustrating roles. Oftentimes, it's both at the same time!" This personal belief and quote of mine is often received with applause from some, blank stares from others, and at least one or two bold women in the room shouting, "AMEN!" The reality of that statement is that I have felt both ends of that spectrum while the truth of it is that out of the eight years of my marriage, three of them were more geared toward the frustrating side. I have discovered that much of that was my fault because I had not understood my role as a wife. I also needed to decide what type of wife I desired and needed to be for my husband.

Many of you, just like myself, entered your marriage with this happily-ever-after mentality. We may have even felt like we didn't need premarital counseling, but because it was a part of Christian culture, we would simply oblige. If you're like me, a divorcee, you may have even had the nerve to say to yourself, "I've done this before, so I'll just purpose to not make the same mistakes, and it will be just fine." Well, if we're honest, that's not exactly the truth.

A personal truth that I have discovered in my marriage is that marriage is definitely the one relationship that will EXPOSE who you really are! It will reveal true character. It will display both your strengths and weaknesses. It will cause you to take a deep look within yourself in order to determine whether it is worth you changing.

At some point during our marriage, we will discover that we may need to make adjustments to ensure a growing and thriving marriage. Not only is that realization eye-opening, but the fact that you as a wife will be the one to make them is important to understand. Yes, marriage is a partnership, and both parties should equally participate in seeing it grow and flourish. But the common truth is that we expect our spouses to change and/or be the ones to change first!

I often made that kind of plea to God in my prayer time. My prayers concerning my marriage were rarely about me changing but about how God needed to change Vincent so that we could have a better relationship. I was so convinced that because he was the man, the head of the household, he needed to change first. I was also convinced that I wasn't doing anything wrong. I obviously was ignoring the signs of my self-righteousness and chose to stay focused on Vincent's sinful ways. Besides, I was the preacher in the home, so in my mind, I was governing my ways according to the Word of the Lord. Surely, God was pleased with me and my actions in this marriage!

As far as I was concerned, my husband had married the perfect woman—not a woman who didn't have flaws, but a woman who had convinced herself that her flaws were not so bad. I also believed that I possessed the skills to mask my flaws at the perfect time. I know I'm not the only woman who thinks or has thought this way, especially considering those of us who are in ministry as speakers, preachers, etc. while our husbands aren't. I am certain of it because I see it too often and have lived it with friends and associates who operated with similar mentalities. I would even be bold enough to say that if you asked the husbands of these women if it were true, they would confirm.

Before I get into the details of what God was specifically dealing with inside my heart, I want to say that even in all of Rome's splendor, it's obvious through the architecture that it took extended periods of time and lots of challenging work for it to become a city that millions would visit! Many are familiar with the well-known idiom: "Rome wasn't built in a day!" For me, this expression serves as a plea for someone to be patient and to not rush the process. This expression also serves as an encouragement that remarkable things or tasks can be accomplished, but they simply take time and invested interest for the task or thing to turn out great! I see how this expression applies to all of our marriages.

As a wife, we must learn to be patient with ourselves, our husbands, and our marriages. Each one of these elements grows and develops in various stages, and the process may take place during different seasons of life.

For example, as a wife, you may have discovered in your marriage that you are more disciplined in your prayer life than your husband. Or you may have discovered that your husband is more disciplined than you in finances. If either of you begin to start badgering the other to be better in those areas where one may not be as strong as the other, it may create dissention, and that will surely cause issues in your union.

Badgering your spouse is another form of nagging or tormenting him. It will never work! As a matter of fact, that behavior will drive your spouse to do the opposite of what you desire out of the marriage. Just a side note ladies, instead of badgering your husband over those areas you see as weaknesses, think along the lines of "purposefully applauding" those areas that you appreciate. Focusing on the positive characteristics dismantles offense as you address the weaknesses with a resolution or suggestion that would benefit you both.

Dissention in marriage causes stress on the relationship that will eventually destroy it. The Bible says in Song of Solomon:

Then you must protect me from the foxes, foxes on the prowl, Foxes who would like nothing better than to get into our flowering garden.
Song of Solomon 2:15 MSG

As the Shulamite verbalizes her love for King Solomon, she speaks of the need to "catch" the foxes that spoil the vines. If the blossoming vineyard is taken to mean the growing romance between the couple, then the foxes represent potential problems that could damage their relationship. This bride-to-be is saying, in essence, "Let's take preventative measures to protect our love from anything that could harm it." I realize that many of us are wives and have already married, but the concept of preventing harmful elements from invading our marriages should be an ongoing process.

In ancient literature, wild animals were often used to represent problems that could separate lovers. Henceforth, dissention could be considered a fox. The three foxes I needed to disrobe in order to be the wife God ordained me to be included my dominating spirit, my unbalanced priorities, and my untamed tongue.

Being married to a dominating or controlling spouse is no fun, but to recognize that I was that person who was carrying that spirit was hurtful. To be strong-willed and determined are great characteristics, but when those characteristics become extreme, they become wicked in the sight of God.

I carried a spirit of Jezebel and didn't recognize it until God directed me to a personal study. I was teaching a Bible study series on the Seven Churches in the book of Revelation. It seemed as if we couldn't move passed the Church of Thyatira. This was the church where Jezebel Doctrine had become acceptable to the Christians in its congregation. As we began to dig into this study, I came across the characteristics of Jezebel, and my heart sank! I couldn't believe that many of these characteristics reflected how I was operating in my marriage. Weeks went by, and the more my class went over Jezebels' characteristics, the more God dealt with my heart.

There are many lists of characteristics that can be researched. Below, I listed the specific ones that I saw in myself that needed to be dealt with. As you read them, it may be difficult to accept that you possess any of the characteristics, but trust me, God will begin to minister to you and expose things about yourself. I remember being in denial at first as well, but the Holy Spirit assured me that I had many of these traits and that it was time to deal with them and get deliverance.

The first step to true deliverance is to be honest about what you see in yourself. I always say, "You can't slay a giant in your life that you're not willing to face." You must acknowledge your issues before you can work to defeat or conquer them! I truly believe that this list was not God's way of condemning me but His way of saving me from my own destruction and saving my marriage.

Excerpt from Confronting Jezebel: Discerning and Defeating the Spirit of Control by Steve Sampson (pages 62-68)

1. **Refuses To Admit Guilt Or Wrong**
   Jezebel spirit is never wrong, unless it is a temporary admittance of guilt to gain "favor" with someone. To accept responsibility would violate the core of insecurity and pride from which it operates. When a Jezebel apologizes it is never in true repentance or acknowledgment of wrongdoing but rather "I'm sorry your feelings were hurt."

2. **Withholds Information**
   This is a form of control. A Jezebel wields power over you by knowing something you don't know in a situation. In the eyes of a Jezebel, having information you don't have is a powerful weapon of control

3. **Ignores People**
   A classic ploy of a controller is to ignore you when you disagree with him/her. This tactic is frequently used by leaders when someone doesn't agree with their plans, and they isolate the person by ignoring him/her. Some in these situations have been ignored for months, just because they chose not to be a puppet and say to every idea or whim. This puts the person out of the leader's grace and forces him/her to either "come around" to the leader's way of thinking or be

indefinitely ignored. One is not free to disagree with a controller.

4. **Criticizes Everyone**
This is a characteristic of a controller. He or she has to be the one who looks good, so he/she will quickly sharply criticize anyone who makes a suggestion or plan. Even though he/she likes the plan, he/she can only criticize it because the idea did not originate from him/her. Criticizing others elevates the controller in his/her own mind.

5. **Is Pushy And Domineering**
A person with a Jezebel spirit pressures you to do things, seemingly ripping from you your right to choose or make a decision for yourself. He or she makes others feel as though they don't have enough sense to think for themselves.

6. **Is Vengeful**
Since a Jezebel is never wrong, if you contradict or confront one, get ready to become his/her worst enemy. As long as you are in agreement with him/her, all is fine. But if you confront or challenge him/her, then look out. You are the target of his/her fiercest venom. A Jezebel will stop at nothing to destroy your reputation

7. **Knows It All**
A Jezebel is usually blatant regarding his/her knowledge of everything. Quick to express his/her opinion in any area, he or she leaves little room for

anyone to point out the other side of an issue. He or she has made idols of his/her opinions.

8. **Is Independent**
   No one has input in a Jezebel's life. He or she fraternizes with no one unless it is to get you to "cooperate" with his/her agenda.

Get rid of all bitterness, rage, and anger, brawling and slander, along with every form of malice. Be Kind and compassionate to one another, forgiving each other, just as Christ God forgave you.
Ephesians 4:31-32 NIV

This Scripture served as a catalyst for helping me rid myself of many of these characteristics. I knew that being controlling was associated with anger, wrath, bitterness, and unforgiveness. Some of my rage and anger could be traced back to my childhood when I was bullied. I also had unresolved issues in a previous relationship where I had experienced domestic violence. These issues followed me into my marriage and had become time bombs waiting to explode.

On the day we decided to view the Colosseum, my dominating spirit decided to show up and almost ruined the experience. Because we hadn't bought tickets in advance, the tour was sold out for the next couple of weeks. My hopes had been to go inside and see every tunnel and every cell that the Gladiators were kept in and to stand in the ruins where the actual fights took place. I was infuriated when we were told there were no tickets. As we walked away, I started yelling at Vincent as if it was all his fault. I was cruel, demeaning, and very belittling. I was even threatening that I wouldn't have any more sex during the trip because he had ruined my childhood dream of seeing the Colosseum. I even began to cry because I was so angry.

As I stormed back into the hotel room, the Holy Spirit arrested me and told me to stop throwing tantrums. I realize that the Holy Spirit is described as a gentleman, but I also believe He speaks to us in a way we all can understand personally. For example, I am a mother of five children, and each of them has a different personality; so my approach is not always the same with all of them when I am addressing situations in their lives. My husband also began to demonstrate Ephesians 4:31-32. The love and compassion he showed me in my moment of self-centeredness was undeserving yet needed. Vincent didn't hesitate to remind me that he could have acted out just as I had, but he chose to show love as the head of the household should. He sternly reminded me that it was my responsibility to purchase the events as he had paid for flights, hotels, and meals. I was convicted, and my Jezebel list popped up in my thoughts. I didn't want to look like that list, so I sincerely apologized to Vincent and repented. As I gathered myself together, we made love.

In the past, I would have withheld sex. Ladies, keep in mind that when we behave this way, we are operating under a spirit of control as we try to manipulate our spouses. The Word of God tells us to not withhold sex from our spouses, especially if it has not been agreed upon by both partners (I Cor. 7:3-7). Instead, I decided to fulfill my husband and simultaneously resist the spirit of control. That was a victory for me!

We ended up walking back to The Colosseum and taking pictures. As we stood there admiring the monumental site, I was reminded that dominance and their will to control was one of the reasons the Romans had ruled for so long in history, but it was also one of the reasons their empire had so many enemies and eventually became their ruin. Their power and need to control led them to make bad military and governmental decisions that weakened them as an empire. I was seeing my own ruin on the horizon with this spirit, so I made the decision to continuously disrobe it when it tries to rear its head.

Having unbalanced priorities in my marriage was another small fox in the vine that needed to be caught. Honestly, my list of priorities was not favorable to my husband's at all. We have five children and I work full-time. I am a writer, a speaker, and a ministry leader in my local church, and these are only a few of the areas of my life that require attention. During a couples counseling session, my husband mentioned that he felt as though everything and everyone took precedence in my life before him. He made mention that ministry, the children, my job, and the church people all made him last on my list, and he resented me and hated being in our marriage because of it. In the past, Vincent had started arguments because of my scheduling, but during that particular session, his words cut like a knife. Hearing my husband say that he resented me and hated being married to me, I was devastated.

I had always been a busy woman, but I didn't realize that my priorities had been so out of balance. I couldn't understand why ministry was going great while my marriage was breaking down. I thought that I was pleasing the Lord by being excellent in ministry and making sure my family was doing well. My children were happy, the church people were happy, and my bosses were pleased, but my husband was miserable. Think about it—I was a woman preaching and ministering the gospel, and my husband was miserable. He wasn't displeased with me doing ministry and all the other things. It was the amount of time and attention that I was giving to these things that caused a problem. It was him feeling like he was getting my leftovers while everyone else was being served to the fullest. Many married women in ministry have this issue and don't recognize it until it's too late. They end up with a thriving ministry but an empty bed!

A false balance is an abomination to the Lord, but a just weight is his delight.

Proverbs 11:1 ESV

God's desire is for us to have a proper balance in our lives. My life and schedule were not only out of balance, but they were out of order. It never dawned on me that in the Christian community where we preach so much about homosexuality, adultery, and greed as an abomination to God, I had never heard a message about God abhorring a false balance as well. God desires for us to live our lives with proper balance, which means we must create boundaries for ourselves. We should put limits in place that keep our scales from tilting over in the wrong direction. What I mean by that is I needed to stop doing so much ministry work and other activities that were preventing me from spending proper time with my husband.

I really struggled with trying to figure out how to make this right in my marriage without it making me miserable and resentful toward Vincent. I loved traveling and ministering at conferences, I loved supporting all the church activities I participated in and coordinated, but I loved my husband more! God ministered to me in prayer one morning, and it put all my fear, worry, and anxiety to rest. This was the order God gave me for creating the balance in my marriage. In chapter nine of my book, *Marriage vs Ministry*, I list what God deposited to me in my spirit.

Here's the order ladies:

1. **GOD = your personal relationship with Him**

2. **Husband = Your FIRST Priority**

3. **Family = Children, parents, friends, etc.**

4. Ministry = Your activities for church, speaking engagements, book writing, prayer lines, etc.

As I meditated on my list, I realized that I had confused my relationship with God with my ministry activities. In so many words, I thought that the more work I did in ministry was my way of demonstrating my relationship with God. Of course, our motive for ministry work should be because we love God and people, but if my home is suffering because of that work, then maybe I'm out of balance with how much of it I am doing.

As a wife, I had to take off my selfishness and see the need of my husband. He needed more time and attention. He needed to feel important to me, and it was my responsibility, not just as a Christian, but as his wife, to put him first—first before my children, first before my ministry, first before my other activities. Many women would fight this process because we live in a time in which women empowerment is on the rise. While this is great, in my opinion, it is out of balance in some areas. I am a woman who believes in empowerment, but not to the point of becominga bossy, overbearing woman who doesn't submit to my husband. One of my favorite Scriptures in Proverbs provides a valuable truth on this matter:

The heart of her husband doth safely trust in her, so that he shall have no need of spoil.

Proverbs 31:14 KJV

I learned that since I've submitted to God's order, my marriage has been amazing, my children are happier, and my ministry is thriving! As a matter of fact, my husband is now working with me on some of my ministry projects and has implemented a youth program that serves the church and community. I believe that when my husband saw me sincerely making the changes to honor him and give him what he needed, he then began to go out of his way to make me happy, and he began to reciprocate by putting me first. Having two people in a marriage who have discovered how to put each other first is part of the recipe for a happy and healthy marriage!

The last of my small foxes that needed to be caught was my untamed tongue. Just the thought of how reckless my mouth was makes me cringe sometimes as I reflect on how far I could take an argument or a simple disagreement between my husband and me. My mouth was lethal and destructive, especially when I felt angry or rejected by Vincent. I didn't know how to communicate effectively to him nor with him. When we didn't agree, to make matters worse, if he walked away from me while having a heated discussion, it would send me through the roof. His silence or what I perceived as a nonchalant attitude pushed me into attack mode. Let me be clear, my husband and I have never exchanged blows in the physical, but our words during arguments hurt just as much!

I remember a heated discussion that started in our bedroom but quickly progressed into our living room area. Front and center, we ended up in each other's faces after I stormed behind him and he walked off. I was screaming so loudly that my son came out of his bedroom to see what fireworks had been set off this time. As my mouth was going one hundred miles per hour and my husband attempted to defend himself, the doorbell rang! I'm sure that the person at the door could hear Vincent and me screaming at the top of our lungs, and they could even view us through the glass portion of our front door. I imagine our unexpected guest was probably terrified as I approached the door.

I quickly gathered my "church girl" attitude—you know the one we have at church or in public, the nice, sweet, chill person we want everyone to think we are 24 hours per day—and I headed to open the door. I was so glad it was only someone who was lost and looking for directions because I was completely embarrassed about the fact that the person had heard us, but at least the individual didn't know us personally. I put a smile on my face, gave the stranger directions, and closed the door quickly with the intent of picking up where I left off with Mr. Speakman. As I turned to resume the argument, my spirit became grieved. An overwhelming feeling of conviction arrested me. I asked myself the question, "What if that had been Jesus at your door, or what if it had been your Pastor who heard you carrying on this way? Would you continue?" The answer was no. But here is the kicker: what made me think it was ok to scream back and forth with my husband that way? Was he not the head of my household, my priest, my "chocolate drop," the one I should be honoring and kind to, even with my words? At that moment, it wasn't about Vincent's actions; it was about me. I had always been taught that God's Word was a mirror to our souls and if that were the case. I was failing miserably! The mirror of God's Word was in my face, and my reflection was not good at all!

When my reflection in my natural mirror is not to my liking, I do what I can to fix it. I'm the same way when it comes to my spiritual reflection. I realized that this "Trigger Lip" that I had was killing my husband's spirit.

Scripture states:

A wise woman builds her home, but a foolish woman tears it down with her own hands.

Proverbs 14:1 NLT

I had been foolish long enough, and I had grown tired of arguing all the time with my husband. My blood pressure was high, I was gaining weight, my focus was off, and I was just very unhappy. Much of these symptoms are associated with stress, and I was too young to be so stressed out! Along with me deciding to execute the Word of God in this area of my life, I found a terrific book that helped me as well. The book, *30 Days to Taming the Tongue*, by Deborah Smith Pegues saved my mouth. I am growing and learning in this area, but I am so much better now, and my husband is so much happier.

Each of my "foxes" are a work in progress. Remember, Rome is a beautiful and spectacular sight to see, but it wasn't built in a day. Be patient with yourself and your spouse as you press into the changes you desire to see. Change in any area always requires a catalyst, and the catalyst usually must endure some discomfort during the change. However, following the process, the results are worth it.

My belief is that as a wife, it is not our job to change our husbands nor is it their jobs to change us. But as a wife, why not be the catalyst to help bring about the desired result? Your desire to see your marriage healthier begins with you becoming a healthier individual. Jacob M. Braude says it like this, "Consider how hard it is to change yourself and you'll understand what little chance you have in trying to change others." A God-fearing wife works on herself and trusts God to work on her husband and her marriage!

POINTS TO PONDER
1. A dominating spirit is witchcraft. Your husband married a woman to have a good wife, not a witch! This level of control is fueled by anger, insecurity, and fear. Its goal is to destroy your marriage!

2. Always strive to give your husband your best, not the leftovers after you've given yourself to everyone else. No spouse wants sloppy seconds, so be sure to make him feel like he is your priority.

3. Always remember that words have power. You can either build your husband up with encouragement or tear him down with criticism. Choose wisely!

POINTS TO PRACTICE
1. In your marriage, learn how to practice "THE PAUSE!" Pause when you're angry. Pause when you're tired. Pause when you're stressed, and definitely PAUSE AND PRAY! Refrain from retaliation and harsh judgment, even when there is a disagreement.
2. Be sure to keep date nights and alone time on your priority list. Spending quality time with your husband makes him feel important. Strive to be sensitive and attentive to his needs. This practice is usually a wonderful way to encourage him to reciprocate the effort.
3. If physically possible, have lots of sex. Sex is a stress reliever and an immune booster. It even lowers your blood pressure along with providing many other benefits. Ladies, you would be surprised to know how kissing, touching, and petting each other can shift the mood—not just for him, but for yourself also.

POINTS TO PRAY
Heavenly Father, bless my sister with insight, wisdom, and peace as she has read this section. Reveal her areas of weakness, and show her how to become accountable to you as you bring deliverance in her areas of need. Bless her

marriage, Father, and continue to align her heart with your Word. Even when facing challenges, Lord, help my sister to have humility, strength, and grace in the process. Teach her how to be the wife that her husband needs so that their marriage may be glorified in You. Renew, revive, replenish, and restore areas in their marriage that they may be influential to other couples. I ask these things in Jesus' name, Amen.

5

From Me to We
Dr. Sakeisha Hylick

These days, American society has drastically shifted in the way people perceive marriage and relationships. While many women spend countless hours and endless amounts of money preparing a wedding that lasts for a day, how many women do you know who actually prepare for a marriage to last a lifetime? Allow me to be transparent with you for a moment. It takes so much more than a pretty face, a banging body, and mind-blowing sex to become a candidate wifehood. Based solely on what you know right now, what do you think being a wife entails? Let me be honest with you. I was clueless. My parents divorced when I was 13 years old, but we had lived in two different states since the time I was four years old. My dad was the deputy warden at Rikers Island Correctional Facility in New York while my mother was an educator at South Carolina State University. I never had the opportunity to witness what a successful marriage entailed, so I based being a wife solely on the brief interactions I witnessed between my parents during the holidays and on my birthday. My grandfather had divorced my grandmother and had a son outside of their marriage who shared my age. My grandfather passed away during his fourth marriage at age 94. My husband's parents had married and divorced each other twice. Ultimately, we didn't have any positive marriages to emulate.

Let's have a moment of total transparency, shall we? I have been with my husband for 25 years now, and we've shared 21 years of marriage. We have seen each other in various stages of life and have been able to celebrate the highs and lows. We have been on mountain tops together and through seasons in the valley together. Have there been times in which I, like many other wives out there, have wanted to walk out the door and call it quits? Absolutely! Yes, I said it! There have been many times, I repeat, many times when I have wanted to pack my bags and say, "Deuces, I am out of here!" It was absolutely nothing but God that kept me from walking out the door. The same goes for my husband. I am sure that as a wife, I have said or done some things that made him want to run for the border.

If you are married or in a serious relationship, take a moment and document the times in which you have had to walk in forgiveness towards your spouse or significant other, specifically in regard to something that they may have said or done that brought about offense, frustration, and disrespect.

One of the things about becoming wife material is learning to transition from "me" to "we." The latter requires a different level of maturity. When you become a wife, the real learning begins. Your mindset must evolve from that of a single woman who is in preparation to become a wife to the mindset of actually being a wife. Keep in mind that this transition doesn't occur overnight. This mindset shift begins once you have realized that you have entered into a new phase of your life. This phase is now a partnership. You have entered into a greater level of commitment. No longer should your focus be solely upon yourself, but now, you have someone else's thoughts, feelings, and life to consider.

When we're intentional about going from "me" to "we," we must be deliberate in not only our words, but in our actions as well. Being intentional in your marriage requires you to be selfless.

Selflessness entails thinking of another person before one's self on purpose. This is a biblical kind of love. Philippians 2:4 tells us to *"look not only to [our] own interests, but also to the interests of others."*

On the journey from "me" to "we," I had to become more selfless and less selfish. As wives, we become more intentional about making the interests of our spouse as important to us as our own individual interests. We need to constantly be in search of ways in which we can learn to enjoy their interests, even if it is not something we thoroughly enjoy. It is also imperative that it be done with a willing heart. When we do, we begin to transform from "me" to "we." During this process, we are both blessed, and our marriage is blessed as well. It's not all about you and your own feelings per se; it's about both of you. Sometimes it is through this process that God is teaching us. It's about appreciating your spouse. It's about building a strong marriage. It's about growing together.

True love is selfless. It is prepared to sacrifice. ~ Author Unknown

Loving our spouse requires that we demonstrate intentional behaviors. Have you ever just taken a look at your spouse and thought really hard of ways you can love him selflessly on a regular basis? It may mean doing some things that you are not particularly fond of, such as watching your husband's favorite sports team for an evening. Once I invested the time to find out what was going on with football, I ended up actually loving to watch the games. We now have something that we can enjoy together, and he is even more apt to watch television shows that I am confident he is not too fond of for my sake. He, too, is learning to become selfless during this process.

    The journey from "me" to "we" may involve watching a movie with your spouse that he selects, even if it is not your ideal movie. It may even involve something such as taking dance lessons when you dislike dancing or trying things outside of your comfort zone. No matter how difficult it may appear to be, being intentionally selfless towards your spouse is a blessing to him and to yourself. It's truly a marriage that can win. It's a win-win situation for the both of you. Just be mindful that it is a process. Just like weight loss is a process that does not transpire overnight, you have to be intentional about the choices you make in regard to food intake and the type of exercise regimen you must incorporate into your daily routine. Likewise, the transition from "me" to "we" takes time.

Did you catch what I said earlier? This transition doesn't take place overnight. It seems as if we have allowed things such as reality TV to somehow distort our way of thinking. Becoming a wife is not a position one should assume lightly.

Answer these questions:
- What does becoming a wife mean from your perspective?
- What have you been taught about being a wife?
- Who taught you these principles?
- Was the person qualified to speak into your life?

I have reasons for asking these questions. Often, men and women enter into the covenant of marriage based on their emotions—how prospects make them feel, how their prospects look, and/or how their prospects treat them. This makes sense, right? But what plan do you have in place for when your spouse is experiencing challenges in his job or in his business? What happens when starts experiencing sexual challenges? What happens when he has emotional challenges? You must consider all of these things when you think about becoming wife material. To be completely honest, I wish that someone had sat me down and discussed this with me.

Becoming a wife can truly be a blessing. Perhaps you are wondering why I am using the word "can." There is no denying the fact that many wives become resentful after marriage when things are not going as anticipated. Things such as financial challenges, job losses, health issues, family influence, and needs of the children, etc. When my husband lost his job the first time, I must admit that I was disappointed. I was pregnant with our first child, and we had just put down thousands of dollars for the construction of our first home. I felt let down, angry, resentful, frustrated, you name it. Notice that I expressed how I felt. It honestly took me a long time to even consider how this may have impacted him. Why? Because I was only thinking about myself. On the journey from "me" to "we," I had to recognize that whatever was impacting me was impacting him as well, and vice-versa.

These issues can eat away at the quality time and attention that you need to devote to one another. This opens the door for the enemy to come in and plant seeds of doubt and frustration. Consider the number of wives you've heard saying, "I didn't know it was going to be like this," or, "I never thought we would wind up like this." Come on—let's be honest with each other. I felt the same way at one point. Then I began to recognize that it was time to flip the script. I began to recognize that instead of the challenges that we faced as a couple, I was going to be intentional and focus on the positive. My marriage was in fact a blessing, and I began to make notes of that. How often has your spouse reminded you of what a blessing you are to him without you even recognizing it?

I can't even begin to tell you how God would put the words in my husband's mouth to say to me at the exact time I needed to hear it the most. He didn't even know how there were so many nights during which I questioned if he loved and appreciated me. It was in the midst of those moments that God would lay on his heart to tell me that how much he appreciated me. He would say little things such as I don't know what I would have done without you! When I felt depleted as if I had done ALL that I know to do and things just didn't look like they were going to work out on my behalf on my job, in my business, in our marriage, Out of the blue he would hug me real tight and whisper in my ear, regardless of what it may look like, he was confident that I can accomplish all that I desired to do. I was the best thing that ever happened to him! Sometimes, he would even send me a quick text with Scripture, and those words penetrated my heart to the point that I knew that God was speaking directly to me through him.

My husband has his own way with expressing himself. His love language is physical touch, while mine is acts of service and words of affirmation, but when prompted by the Holy Spirit, I recognize exactly what he's saying, even if his choice of words isn't what I expected.

He who finds a [true and faithful] wife finds a good thing and obtains favor and approval from the Lord.
Proverbs 18:22 AMP

If the covenant that you are about to enter results in favor and approval from God, then trust me, it is not something to be entered into lightly.

Qualities of Wife Material

She Expresses What She Expects Effectively! Your husband is not able to read your mind. Your thoughts and decisions no longer impact just you, but they directly impact the one that is connected to you, your spouse. Keep in mind that neither one of you are perfect, even though you may feel like you are. I admit, I thought that I was perfect in the sense that I blamed everything on him. A spouse whose needs are not being met will often result in frustration, which often leads to resentment.

Additionally, when moving from "me" to "we," be mindful that your expectations need not be unattainable. Often times, your spouse may have expectations that have been set from previous relationships and are truly unrealistic, and as a result, it places undue pressure on your current spouse.

Allow me to clarify what I mean by the term, "unrealistic expectations." As women, we typically see our spouses as a project. We think," Oh, I can fix this about him," or "I can change that about him," and when it doesn't turn out as anticipated, we feel let down and frustrated.

When I met my husband, I saw him as a project. He was an amazing guy, he kept me laughing, and we always enjoyed each other's company. However, he didn't dress the way that I thought he should dress, his speech wasn't as polished as I thought it should be, and he wasn't as knowledgeable about real estate as I was. All of those realities frustrated me.

After a serious disagreement one night, he told me that I needed to "go and pray." So I went into the bathroom, slammed the door, and began to cry out to God, complaining about this imperfect man that He had given me. This went on for several nights in a row. In that place, God began to remind me of all the ways in which my husband had loved me despite all of my imperfections, my wrongdoings, and my selfish acts. I came out of that bathroom, still angry, wondering why God was taking my husband's side. Couldn't God see how his actions were impacting me? I had some serious issues to address. Yet God loved me so much that He even touched my husband's heart and allowed him to recognize that his wife was hurting, not because of him, but because of my past hurts and disappointments. I was just taking it out on my husband.

I love God so much. He knew exactly what I needed in order to go from "me" to "we." When I walked out of the bathroom that night, my husband took me by the hand, led me to the couch, and said that he would not be a true man of God if he spent all of his time pouring into others and praying for them without giving the same dedication to his wife. He said if we needed to stay up ALL NIGHT until we resolved the issue, then he was willing to do it even though he was exhausted because our marriage being intact was worth way more to him than a few extra hours of sleep. He was not going to rest until this was resolved. I was astounded at this point. My heart began to melt. Heavy weights and burdens began to fall off of me. God demonstrated that He had given me the husband that I needed, and it was time for me to take a look in the mirror and see what adjustments I needed to make in order to go from "me" to "we." This journey from "me" to "we" is not an easy one, but it is definitely worth it.

Here are some of those common, unrealistic expectations:

A) **We Will Never Have Challenges**

Challenges are going to arise in any relationship. God does not expect us to be perfect, but we must work through the process. We must surrender the need for perfection. Otherwise, we begin to carry excess weight of responsibilities that we weren't meant to carry.

B) **We Will Never Be Tempted**

Temptation in marriage comes in many different forms, not just sexual temptation. Each person has their own love language, and when a spouse is not meeting that need as another person steps in and begins to provide that need, it opens up the door for the enemy to move in. When you notice this, it's time to have a meeting with your spouse and let him know how you are feeling and what you would like to see from him. This does not guarantee an overnight transformation by any means, but what it does do is plant the seed.

C) My Spouse Will Never Let Me Down

We are all imperfect beings who make mistakes. Even though we may have the best intentions, we all fall short at one time or another. The same grace that God extends to us daily should be extended to our spouse. You must understand that Your spouse was not created to meet your every need. Like many wives, I often found myself thinking or believing "in my own feelings" when my spouse didn't meet all of my needs. I had to step back from the situation and reverse the roles. How would I want to be treated if the shoe was on the other foot? Was I even living up to what I was expecting from him?

D) We Will Always Be On The Same Page

Sorry. We are all created in God's likeness, but we were not created to be mirrored images of one another. What makes a wife a successful one is her ability to recognize how she is different from her spouse and use her gifts and talents to be a blessing to the marriage. There are going to be times in which the two of you are not going to see eye to eye, and that is okay. Have the conversation and see how to navigate that situation with the understanding that the two of you are not always going to agree, but be open to hearing his perspective. Then, move forward.

It is important to take a step back to re-evaluate your needs, and then consider if your spouse may actually be able to meet them. Maybe your spouse isn't where you are financially. Work on appreciating what the two of you do have instead of what you don't have.

Helpful Advice for the "Me" to "We" Transition:

1) **Pick and choose your battles wisely because your words carry weight.**

Constant criticism can eat at the very fiber of your relationship. When tensions rise, it is very easy to operate from a posture of high emotions and low intelligence. On the journey from "just me" to "we," your hurtful words can cause your spouse to erect a wall as a form of protection. Once this wall goes up, it will require twice as much time and effort to tear it down, so choose your battles wisely. When you are facing what appears to be one of those uphill battles in your marriage, go to GOD (our Father, Creator, Maker of Heaven and Earth), the One who has all of the answers. You will be surprised at how many high-spirited debates and arguments can be resolved using Godly wisdom rather than resorting to fleshly responses.

2) **Establish and maintain boundaries within your marriage.**

As a single woman, your friends and family members may have been the first person that you called when there were challenges in your life. Once you have entered the journey of the two of you becoming one, your spouse should be your first go-to person. With that being said, be mindful of the discussions you have with family and friends regarding your relationship with your spouse. Resist the urge to demoralize or speak ill of your spouse with your friends and/or your family. Additionally, refrain from joining in conversations that involve your friends and/or family members saying negative things about your spouse. This opens up the door to disloyalty. Your primary loyalty is to your spouse, not to your family, friends, co-workers, or even social media. We all know what role social medium has begun to play in our relationships. Social media and technology have been responsible for the embarrassment, humiliation, and ultimate destruction of many relationships.

3) Don't try to change your spouse into who YOU feel they should be.

On the journey from "me" to "we," it is imperative to accept your spouse who he is and not according to how you feel he should be. Take a step back from the situation and consider this question. Would you want your spouse to try to change you? Think of it according to the following Scripture:

Husbands, love your wives [seek the highest good for her and surround her with a caring, unselfish love], just as Christ also loved the church and gave Himself up for her
Ephesians 5:25 AMP

The Bible clearly states that a husband should love his wife just as Christ loved the church. God loves us as we are. We, in turn, are to demonstrate the same level of love towards our spouse. It is imperative that we love our spouses as they are and let them know that we would never want them to change in any way to earn our love. Our spouses have so much to offer us, but we must allow them to be themselves. On the journey from "me" to "we," it is essential that we treat our spouses with the same level of respect that we want from them. Marriage is a work in progress. We are all constantly growing and changing. Therefore, being a wife will require us to realize that marriage is a constant learning process.

To take it one step further on this journey from "me" to "we," another important task is to accept that you and your spouse are individuals. You are not created to be mirrored images of one another. We are only created to reflect God's image. Because of this, you and your husband won't always see the world from the same perspective, and that's a good thing. Being with someone who isn't exactly like you will open your eyes and make your relationship richer.

There's a difference between asking your husband to pick his clothes up off the floor or to do the dishes and asking him to go hiking when he obviously hates the outdoors. You can ask him to improve in different areas, but you must be willing to give the same level of commitment. Remember, you can't force him to like all of the same things that you like, but you must consider his feelings and be willing to try some of his interests as well. Remember, it's not just about you anymore, but it's about the two of you building a life together on this journey.

4) **Be willing to adapt and change**

As a married woman on this journey, you will encounter various types of crises together. My husband and I have learned to lean on one another during the loss of a job, the death of my father, and as our mothers-in-law experienced a decline in health. Change is something that is constant. I'd like to share another moment of transparency with you. My husband and I had to learn to adapt in so many ways. As an only child of a retired deputy warden in Rikers Island and a retired educator/entrepreneur, finances were never an issue in our household. The word "budget" wasn't a part of my vocabulary. Fast forward to my marriage at a point when we had our first financial challenge. I was taken aback. After having never experienced a financial problem, I suddenly found myself in a place where I had just graduated from pharmacy school, I was pregnant with our first child, we had just placed a sizeable deposit down to build our first home, and then the unexpected happened— my husband was laid off. The funny thing was that I could no longer think about how this was going to impact me, but how it was going to impact us. The journey is not just mine; it is ours.

Lesson Learned

As a couple, you and your spouse may encounter financial hardships. You may find yourselves experiencing health challenges and intimacy issues, and quite frankly, you may feel unsure of what to do. Please know this. Your marriage can survive the challenges placed before you if you remember that the two of you are on the same team. You are no longer by yourself. It's essential to do these two things:
- Keep the lines of communication open.
- Remain flexible.

Here are some things to be mindful of:
On this journey, there may be changes that take place in one or both of you physically, emotionally, financially, etc. Remember that whatever happens on this journey from "me" to "we," you and your spouse are designed to complement one another and not compete with one another. Dealing with the challenges together as a team makes it a much more manageable undertaking.

POINTS TO PONDER

A woman that is wife material on the journey from "me" to "we" recognizes that she must be equipped to walk in the following areas:
- The ability to forgive
- The ability to trust
- The ability to be vulnerable
- The ability to be flexible
- The ability to grow in her relationship with God

A relationship is a partnership capable of enhancing every aspect of your life, emotionally, mentally, physically, spiritually, and sexually. Each couple is different, and there are no hard and fast rules to developing a healthy relationship. The key is for both partners to invest time and effort in keeping the relationship strong, vibrant, and moving forward. A journey from "me" to "we" needs to be active, dynamic, and engaging.

POINTS TO PRACTICE
1) **Plan**

Premarital counseling is a must. Just like getting a driver's license or a pharmacist license, I needed to have an understanding of what's expected of me as a wife, the kinds of tests I may encounter or challenges that I will have to overcome. As we discussed earlier, challenges are to be expected in any relationship, but like any job or any business endeavor, you must consider what measures you have implemented to ensure that this relationship is successful.

2) **Prepare**

Before you can be a wife, you must be confident in who you are as a person. My husband and I knew a wife who had several different medical issues and constantly used that as a means to continuously lean on her spouse. Why am I mentioning this? Well, some people tend to believe that in a marriage, two halves make a whole; however, you and your husband must be complete individuals before the two of you can truly become one. In order to prepare a meal, don't you need to have the ingredients? If you only have some of this and a little of that, you are preparing for one big mess. Do you clearly understand your expectations? Has your husband communicated his needs, his likes, and his dislikes? Do you even know all of that about yourself? Can you communicate them clearly, effectively and honestly? Preparation is key.

3) Pray Scriptures Daily

There is no more powerful tool to have in your arsenal than prayer. The two of you need to make prayer a normal part of your daily routine. Let's be real, marriage is no easy task. These days, people are getting married for all of the wrong reasons. What happens when the finances dry up due to a job loss, or you face a health challenge that was unexpected? When you realize that your marriage is not what you thought it was and your

needs are not being met, what is your response? Cover yourself and your spouse in prayer daily. Trials may come. Temptation may come. One Scripture that I stand on and truly recommend is the following:

"For I know the plans and thoughts that I have for you," says the Lord, "plans for peace and well-being and not for disaster, to give you a future and a hope."
Jeremiah 29:11 AMP

So whenever a challenge arises, I run to my Bible and read this Scripture before I do anything else. God is always speaking to us, but are we always listening? You need to position yourself to hear from Him so that your marriage can win.

4) Position Your Marriage to Win
- Your spouse needs to know that they are your number one priority, second only to

God. Your spouse needs to feel more important than your business, your job, your kids, your parents, your friends, and anything that takes your time and attention. Prioritize—God first, then your spouse—no exceptions.

For this reason a man shall leave his father and his mother, and shall be joined to his wife; and they shall become one flesh.   Genesis 2:24 AMP

God should always be the first one that you consult during any challenge in your marriage. The first earthly person that you go to should be your spouse, not your mother, father, siblings, or best friends, etc. God will never steer you wrong!

- Respect him by letting him be the man. Utilizing insults in an attempt to motivate him to change can backfire and be counterproductive. Make it a point to acknowledge and praise his accomplishments both inside and outside of the home. Reassure him of how valuable he is to your life.

- Create a safe space for open and emotionally honest dialogue to happen. Connect with him in a way that allows him to come to you with concerns in every area of his life, be it home, family, work, or outside interests. Don't shut him out.

5) **Persevere**

Some days are more challenging than others. Some days, my husband and I don't see eye to eye. Yet, I know that God brought us together, and I know God's desire is for us to persevere. I pray for endurance. I pray for understanding. I pray for humility and grace to abound in our hearts in Jesus' name, AMEN!

a) If you are tempted to give up, I encourage you to start by remembering your promise to love your spouse for better or for worse. Even though we don't like to focus on the "worse," it happens, but it is not an indication that the marriage should end.
b) Be willing to seek help. Connect with other godly couples who can help keep you accountable to each other and to God. You may be faced with tough times, but don't give up.

Here's some advice that has helped me in doing this.

- **Make the necessary adjustments in your schedule** to spend quality time with your spouse, and do things that both of you enjoy. Your marriage is a work in progress. It cannot be solely about what you want, but it should be about what both of you want and need.

- **Establish boundaries with in-laws and friends.** Remember, others can only become as involved in your relationship as the two of you permit. What transpires in your household is not just your business, but it is your husband's as well. That's why it is important for the two of you to agree on what information is to be shared with those outside of your home. When it was just you, it may have been acceptable to have friends and relatives drop by unannounced; however, it is now the two of you, and your spouse's feelings need to be taken into consideration as well.
- **Recognize the power of the word "NO."** There are going to be things that come up continuously that will rob you and your spouse of your time together. The two of you have to be intentional about guarding your marriage from time stealers. Do not overcommit to things that cause you to constantly be worn out and wind up giving your spouse what is left over.
- **Remember that "you can't pour from an empty cup!"**

POINTS TO PRAY

As I close out this topic, I just want to take a moment to encourage each woman who is reading this book right now and is maybe struggling in her marriage or isn't sure whether to stay or to go. I encourage you to take the next few minutes and seek honestly to hear God's voice in regards to your situation. I pray that God gives you the kind of peace that surpasses all understanding according to Philippians 4:7.

I pray for divine wisdom and strategies on how to successfully navigate the institute of marriage. I pray for divine health and strength to endure and overcome any challenges that may come you way. May God help you to walk boldly as a woman, a wife, and a child of the Most High God. I pray that you will experience God's love. May you have the type of peace and joy that comes only from having an intimate relationship with God.

Lord, I pray that her prayers sustain her husband and that she will be a light to other women who have also faced similar challenges. Be her rock and support in those times when she may become weary of well-doing according to Galatians 6:9. Finally, Father, help her to stand on Jeremiah 29:11: "For I know the plans and thoughts that I have for you,' says the Lord, 'plans for peace and well-being and not for disaster, to give you a future and a hope."

Father, you have a plan for her and for her marriage. Help her to recognize it and walk fully thereof. Cover her and bless her from the crown of her head to the soles of her feet. Help her to recognize that there is no weapon formed against her that shall prosper. In Jesus' name, I pray. Amen.

6
How We Made It Through the Storm
Carol Simpson

He was hooked on food. I was hooked on ministry. We were both addicted to what we each believed, and it felt good to us. We were blinded by the fact that we wanted what we wanted. It wasn't until we allowed the revelation of God to come in that we recognized we were messed up. If our marriage was going to survive, we needed a change.

Laying in the cut (my prayer time), there was something that I needed to realize before change could truly come. Having to admit I was the one that needed to change was a challenge, but I wanted it bad, so I bowed down to it. In His presence, God zeroed in on me. I didn't want to confess to Him that I had the issues because I wanted my husband to be the responsible party—only him.

I realized that in order for resolution to come when the problem is identified, there must be admission and acceptance of truth. WIVES, we usually want it to be the husband who admits his issues, and that's ok, but we must be willing to get down to the root of the problem even if it is because of us. This is how the marriage is going to get better and survive the storm.

God told me to take off my "divinity" and put on my "humanity." At first, I didn't get it, but then God led me to the Word.

Therefore shall a man leave his father and his mother, and shall cleave unto his wife: and they shall be one flesh.
Genesis 2:24 KJV

This Scripture clearly indicates who we should leave and cleave to. This answer is each other, not others or ministry! Divinity is connected to things above, and humanity is connected to the things on earth. While marriage is a spiritual thing, it is also an activity here on earth.

The Bible clearly gives us instructions for marriage in I Corinthians:

There is a difference also between a wife and a virgin. The unmarried woman careth for the things of the Lord, that she may be holy both in body and in spirit: but she that is married careth for the things of the world, how she may please her husband.

I Corinthians 7:34 KJV

The union of marriage is in the flesh first, then the Lord gives us instructions through His Word regarding how to build a relationship with each other and with Him. However, we often make it so "SUPER" spiritual that we become no "EARTHLY" good, as the old folks taught me. As a wife, we must know that God's institution of marriage requires human-to-human contact on earth with each other, so I need to fulfill the requirements.

We are spirit *and* flesh, and sometimes the flesh part is forgotten as we forget our commitment to our husbands. That's where the problems begin. A man will tolerate your "divinity" to an extent, but at some point, you better put your "humanity" on and just be his wife!

How the Storm Began

I learned this principle well through trial and error being that I was married young and both my husband and I were heavily involved in church. We were committed to the ministry, and the Lord began to pull on my heart about the call He had on my life.

As I worked in the ministry and wore several hats because the ministry was still small at the time, I loved ministering Jesus to people and winning them for the Kingdom of God. It gave me such pleasure and an adrenaline rush to see the Word of God operate in my life. Luke 15 says it best:

Likewise, I say unto you, there is joy in the presence of the angels of God over one sinner that repenteth.
Luke 15:10 KJV

The brewing started as God began to thrust me outside of the ministry as an evangelist after I had made my election sure to my leaders. I called my pastor and asked him to lay hands upon me. Before I went out, he instructed me to attend midday prayer where he would lay hands on me as another minister witnessed it. This verse from Luke 4 was evident:

The Spirit of the Lord God is upon me; because the Lord hath anointed me to preach good tidings unto the meek; he hath sent me to bind up the brokenhearted, to proclaim liberty to the captives, and the opening of the prison to them that are bound.
Luke 4:18, KJV

I had been bitten by the "ministry bug." The Bible tells us this:

Do not be anxious about anything, but in every situation,

by prayer and petition, with thanksgiving, present your requests to God.   *Philippians 4:6 NIV*

I did hear and consult God, but somewhere in the process, I took a wrong turn, which started a storm in my marriage. I was determined to obey God to the fullest, but in many ways, I began to neglect my husband and family.

During this time, my husband began to gain an astronomical amount of weight. He had always been a well-disciplined man, but something was off. I knew we had been called to ministry, and God confirmed that we were pastors. I began to get angry at my husband as I questioned how we would fulfill God's calling on our life if he couldn't even stand up.

I found out later that he became equally angry with me because I was traveling all over the place, preaching and ignoring him and the family. Even though in my heart, I loved my family dearly, I was blinded by my love for ministry. The lack of a decent balance presented serious danger in my marriage.

We continued down this dangerous path, and we became angrier and angrier with each other. Then, we both begin to act out of character with one another, forgetting the vows we had taken before God and the commitment, we had made to each other.

The Process

My husband and I would pick up people for church and stuff them into our car along with our three children as we looked for all types of ways to increase the ministry for the glory of God. We found pleasure in doing it, but we were going through many challenges in our marriage at the same time.

My husband was given a position by the Pastors to be the church's Chief Financial Officer, and that was cool. He was diligent and faithful to the task, and I began to get angry about that because I felt he was more committed to the position and to the church than he was to his own body, marriage, and family. As a result, the anger was constantly compounded on both sides, and the devil was using it to the fullest.

My husband continued to gain weight and seem unconcerned about other things, including me. At the same time, I was still out preaching and serving in the ministry there along with my husband. However, I began to be mistreated in the ministry. They seemed to love my husband, but they would not be so nice to me. That experience made me even angrier to be a part of a ministry that only loved one of us though we were both being faithful in every area. Nevertheless, we believed in order, so we were obedient to God and submitted to our leaders.

Because we were leaders and wanted to be good examples before others, we made sure our pastors were informed when we missed church and when I was out preaching in order to avoid conflict in the ministry.

After joining the ministry, our leaders found out that my husband and I were called to be pastors within four months, but we never changed our character or moved out of a position to serve. It was not our time yet. We loved God, we loved our leaders, and we loved their vision. We just wanted to help them accomplish their goals at all costs, so we made significant sacrifices.

It was in this season that I felt I was being mistreated, first by the pastor's wife and eventually from him as well. Again, anger grew within me because I felt my husband was not protecting me, and there is nothing worse than the feeling of not being protected by one's husband. When I expressed my feelings to him, it seemed as though he could not hear me at all, and the abuse continued.

The weight gain, me being on the road, and the bad treatment from the ministry that I was experiencing caused a lot of trouble in our marriage. Our communication was totally off, and I wanted "out." He wanted "out" too. Yet we kept that to ourselves, believing that if we had spoken it out loud in the open, the devil would use it to break us up. We were fighting to hold on to each other even though we were broken, not to mention our sex life was a total wreck.

My husband had gained up to 587 pounds and was totally depressed, and I was as mad as ever. I had a dream through which God told me that my husband was going to get the gastric bypass surgery and everything would be fine. This prophecy was hard for me to believe because my husband was a man who could not ever tolerate any type of major pain, but I believed God, pushed past my own human feelings, and trusted the Lord at His word.

He had gone to the doctor prior to this incident and was told that if he kept playing golf, he would be paralyzed. That news depressed him further because he LOVED playing golf from sunup to sundown. It was his great escape.

One day, my husband went to the grocery store, and when he returned, he said, "I fell on the ground. My knees buckled, and I just went down." We both became concerned. The following morning, he went to Urgent Care. Even though he was frightened, he knew it was time to see what was going on.

He was referred to a brain specialist after the fall, so we went there to see if we could identify the problem. The doctor began to tell him that he had some type of brain injury that caused his knees to buckle. We left there, and he began to cry because the doctor made it seem as though he was going to need brain surgery. It WAS NOT a good diagnosis.

Our son who was eight or nine at the time was with us, and he began to prophesy to his dad and tell him, "there is nothing wrong with your brain, and God said you are going to be just fine." We just began praising God, for out of the mouth of a babe, God had spoken.

We then went to a primary doctor. We will never forget how honest, pure, and helpful she was. She spoke to my husband and said, "Sir, you are too big, and you must get your mind together and consider having the gastric bypass surgery if you want to live. I have viewed your x-rays, and there is nothing wrong with your brain, but you are borderline diabetic with hypertension. And other things are going on in your body because of the weight. Let's start this journey to get you back to health, and if you want to live, you will do what I'm instructing you to do."

I suggested to my husband that we both go on the Atkins diet because he had to be below 500 pounds to get the surgery, so he and I both began to mellow out some. I started to see the need for me staying in town and taking care of him and the family. As a result, things began to calm down in our marriage.

He immediately lost 40 to 50 pounds after coming off soda and eating less candy, and that encouraged him tremendously. At the time, he used a cane. We lived in a two-story house, and he was in lots of pain at all times. Nevertheless, he continued to go to work and never complained about it because he had made my mom a promise that he would always take care of the kids and me. I was thankful for that because God had removed me from my job, and I didn't know why.

Our marriage continued to suffer until, one day, I was running past the bathroom as my husband was in the shower, and I heard God say, "Take your clothes off, go into the shower, and help him because he cannot bathe himself." So I obeyed.

Once I entered the shower and told him what God said to me, he broke down and began to sob and weep, and so did I. He said, "Honey, I've been in here for months not able to shower myself properly." The next process of the storm had begun in our broken and fractured marriage. God was bringing restoration and healing back into it.

How I Endured The Storm

After that day in the shower, something on the inside of my spirit happened. God had begun to answer my prayers about my marriage. I immediately sprang into action to nurse my man back to health, and as the process continued, the Spirit of the Lord helped me to endure the storm.

I had to begin bathing him every day, two times per day—once at 4:30am, and once at 7pm. I only focused on taking care of my husband, my marriage, and my family. Our perceptions of God, of each other, and of our marriage had changed. It was as if God had taken the blinders off our eyes like He had done for Samson, and He began to give us a second chance to destroy the things that had us in bondage.

It was then that our communication opened up once again, and we stopped displaying negative behavior toward one another. We discussed everything, and we were open to see and hear the issues we had with one another without being defensive.

On one occasion while I was bathing my husband, he slipped and fell backwards, busting the wall in the shower and leaving a big, gaping hole. This required us to go downstairs and do his bathing twice a day. The devil tried everything to discourage me, but his tactics did not work. We stayed focused on what needed to be done.

Once, the devil even told me to look at my hands because I had calluses all over them, but I said, "Devil, I'll use some Vaseline to soften them up because you will NOT stop me from nursing my man back to health." God had a purpose for us, so I continued, and the devil stopped talking. We are told to resist the devil and he will flee, and he did just that.

During the process of nursing my husband back to health, there were times when I felt like I was at my lowest, but somehow, God came through. He empowered me to feel His encouragement and pushed me and enabled me to conquer the task that had been put upon me. I knew the Holy Spirit was working on me because through natural eyes and natural circumstances, I would have reacted with negative feelings and emotions and aborted the assignment.

People that knew the inside scoop looked on in amazement because, after all, they had witnessed my pain and the turn of events. Though I was trying my hardest to be a trooper, there were days in which I felt like it was just too much. One day, I was SO depressed, and I was upstairs in the bed crying uncontrollably. My husband asked me what was wrong, and I could not even answer.

My husband took immediate action and called my sister and mom. They came over and ran upstairs, and my sister sprang into action as she began to go into warfare and lay hands on me. I immediately began to calm down and come back to myself. I had been overtaken by my situation that had been ongoing for over ten years.

Back in my right mind, I realized that I had never seen my sister do that before. Because she was put in that position, it released something within her, and she has not been the same ever since. I thank God for using her that day. It changed my life and hers! So please know that when you are submitted to God, even your pain can serve as an opportunity to push people into greatness.

We had to call a plumber along with other professionals to handle the broken wall in the shower. We found out there was mold behind the wall, and this significantly increased the price for the repairs. We needed that money along with the money for my husband's surgery, which was a $10,000 co-pay. Let me tell you that the Lord provided! Remember, I was not employed, and we were living on one income at the time after having been accustomed to two incomes.

Shortly after making the decision to help bathe my husband, he had to have the assistance of two canes in order to walk. He was also having a very difficult time functioning in his job because he could not walk far, and that also became a problem. Yet, the Lord had him and sent help to get his job done so that he could continue to work and provide for his family.

With my husband still having to rely on two canes, we were preparing for his surgery. He had lost weight and was under 500 pounds. I still had calluses all over my hands. As we entered the hospital, I knew he was very afraid, but I assured him along with family and friends that he was going to be okay because the Lord was going to see him through. I had previously shared with him that I had about him getting the surgery and that I saw him come through perfectly. He received it, and the doctors put him under.

After the surgery, the doctors told him he could not be released from the hospital until all of his vitals were good, and of course he had a high fever, so that added more days to his stay. He was frightened and asked me if I was going home, and I said, "No, honey. I packed clothes in order to stay in the hospital with you." That gave him so much comfort.

After returning home, we decided to take the walk up the steps since we had gotten the upstairs bathroom repaired. We had to follow the strict instructions of the doctors for bariatric patients. That meant that everything he ate had to be measured and could not ever be altered. He still had to be bathed and nursed back to health, so in the middle of the night, he would awaken me several times because he would have to use the restroom. He would also be in pain, so he needed more medication.

We also had to be careful with the pain medication because it was statistically proven that a lot of bariatric patients were becoming addicted to the pain medication, and that brought on a whole other set of problems. We had known some people had become addicted to the medication and died as a result.

It was this experience that taught me another level of ministry, though I had always considered myself a servant. Seeing my husband in his most vulnerable state birthed a compassion that is necessary to bring people through real recovery. This was another level of submission I acquired in the marriage as a wife.

The surgery required a lot of patience, sacrifice, and work for it to be successful, but we were determined to see it through and to do everything the doctors had instructed us to do. The first couple of days, my husband could only have yogurt and soft eggs. My life for that moment had changed because I had to endure the process, and I never hesitated to do what needed to be done. I just sprang into action because this was my husband, and God had a promise over his life. I knew that we needed to work as a team in order to accomplish it! This ordeal required us to walk out the Word of God at a greater rate than anything I had ever experienced.

We must bear the infirmities of the weak. The same way God carried me in my frail state, He was extending the same privilege to me. I had just come out of a 13-year trial, yet I had a "let's get this" mentality because I had my man back, and God was using this situation to transform both of our minds. After about two weeks, my husband had lost 50 to 70 pounds, and he looked and felt good. He no longer relied on the canes, but he kept one just to make sure his balance was good.

How I Came out of the Storm with the Victory

My husband returned to work, and people that had not seen him in years said, "Man, I thought you were dead or had been fired." It was difficult for him to leave and get his lunch because of his physical ailments. Seeing his need, one of his co-workers decided to do it for him. God even blessed him in providing a co-worker who drove him to and from work. This was a true blessing because he worked one hour and 45 minutes away from where we lived in Vegas.

We began to go on dates again and communicated even better than before. We began to love on each other to make up for the opportunities we had missed due to being angry and bitter. While lying in bed, my husband repented to me for ALL he had done and began to tell me he knew he had been in bondage to food. He told me that he was going to make it up to me. I also repented to him for my shenanigans of running around in ministry and putting him and the family second.

Those negative behaviors cost us a whole lot in our marriage, and we suggest to everyone reading our story that you give thought to your decisions before you make them. Count up the cost and do your homework because it may not turn out good. We know some couples that have divorced over putting the ministry before each other, and now they have nothing.

It's extremely important that couples have a prayer life, a digestion of the Word, and a relationship with God first before having a relationship with each other. Once negative things begin to happen in your marriage, you need something to pull from, but if you go in with this principle, your marriage is not going to fail unless you get careless.

The Bible tells us that we have victory in the book of Revelation:

And they overcame him by the blood of the lamb, and by the word of their testimony; and they loved not their lives unto the death.

Revelation 12:11 KJV

That's why I am giving my testimony of how we made it through the storm. We have overcome and weathered the storm together. Now, we are walking in Victory!

Just as God made a promise to Joseph when he gave him the dream of who he would become, the Lord had told us in 1989 that we were pastors. At the time, we certainly did not want to be pastors, but through the process, God softened our hearts. We received the word of the Lord, and now we are pastors here in Las Vegas at Shekinah Glory Ministries.

When I made a decision as a wife to submit my ways to the Lord, He began to turn things completely around for me. I made a decision that my marriage was what I wanted the most, not rocking the mic in front of folks that would shout, scream, and run as they got delivered when I needed deliverance in my own home.

In reading this story, some may wonder why I've placed the focus more heavily on my husband than on myself. It was on purpose because in marriage, your husband's struggles are your struggles and vice versa. In order to walk through a process that you don't think you deserve or believe could have been avoided if it had been a "solo project," you must surrender to a greater love. Marriage is truly the two becoming one.

Everything merges. My struggles are my husband's, and his are mine.

This surrender birthed balance. I decided to have balance and take off my divinity and put on my humanity to PLEASE my husband, which brought glory to God because that is His order according to the Word of God. Even while I was set on wanting my own way, I prayed many times that God would revive, restore, and renew my marriage. I also asked Him to fulfill the word of the Lord that had been spoken over us many years ago.

My husband and I both rejoiced in the Lord "for He is good and His mercies endureth forever," according to Psalm 136:1. As the Lord's promises over our lives are being fulfilled, we are so much happier in every area. Every day is not the best, but the past is behind us.

I press toward the mark for the prize of the high calling of God in Christ Jesus.
Philippians 3:14 KJV

We are 37 years in and still walking the promise out, but we are nowhere near where we used to be. The Lord has used all of our shortcomings, failures, and mistakes to bless other marriages, and that's what it's all about—no pain, no gain. We have been in the pit and in the prison, and now we are headed to the palace.

POINTS TO PONDER
The order of God for Ministry:

1. Your relationship with God
2. Your relationship with each other as Husband/Wife
3. Your relationship with your kids
4. Your livelihood—how you will make money to survive
5. The Ministry

POINTS TO PRACTICE
1. Make it a practice to pray together and discuss what the Lord has revealed to you

   both, and be honest, even if it's negative. Always speak your truth with love.

2. DO NOT keep any secrets, even if you're mad at each other. In Ephesians 4:26, the Bible clearly says, "Be angry, and sin not: let not the sun go down upon your wrath."

3. COMMUNICATE with each other, and keep others opinions out if it's not good council!

POINTS TO PRAY

1. Marriage is being a team, which means no outside voices.

2. What does God want from us/our purpose?

3. Who are we called to? Ask God to define it so you stay in your lane.

Do your homework, and know the value and consequences of your decision.

7
Different Requires Different
Elois Wash

My mother married once and has been separated for over twenty years. She never remarried. My mother in-law was married five times and divorced all five times. As I entered the union with my spouse, we did not have a good example to model for our own marriage. However, I knew I wanted to have a successful marriage. Because I did not have a tool in place, I looked up to what society believed a good marriage should be. I came up with a list of unrealistic beliefs, which I thought was going to create a successful marriage. I wanted my marriage to be different than what I had seen, so I had to do it differently. Thinking it would bring me success, I tried to mimic my list in my marriage. After years of implementing these ideas into my marriage, I realized they were not working. I had to make some changes in order to focus on the specific needs of my partner rather than statistics if I wanted my marriage to work.

Be Careful of Your Past

Your past can play a major role in your marriage. In my case, it impacted my marriage in a negative way. Selfishness was one of the things I have dealt with in my marriage. Although selfishness was not my intention, I found it very difficult for me to not put my own desires before my spouse. Growing up, I was an only child for several years. Being an only child, I got everything I wanted from my parents. In addition to getting things from my parents, I also received from my aunties and other relatives who did not have any children. This played a role in my inclination to prioritize my own needs. As a result, I was very settled in my ways. As a child, I did not want to share anything with anyone, and if it was not catering to my wants and needs, then I was not interested in being involved. I noticed I carried the same selfish behavior into my marriage.

My past affected my relationship with my husband. Something that had happened to me at a young age caused my marriage to suffer. Being reared by my grandmother, I had a relative who violated me as a child. Because of that, I avoided doing many things with my husband. My husband liked to cuddle, but I would not cuddle with my husband. My husband loved to kiss, but I would not kiss my husband because it reminded me of the time that my innocence was taken. Furthermore, he used to tell me he loved me, but I could not bring myself to say it back to him. In spite of my selfishness, my spouse was very selfless. He never treated me differently due to my issues. He remained faithful while believing things would change.

Always Show Support

Perspective was one important role that could not be ignored in my marriage. Having come from different backgrounds, my outlook was very different from my husband's. He saw things one way, and I saw things a different way, which really affected our marriage. I knew support was important to my spouse, so I was showing support the way I knew how. Being the preacher's wife, praying was a major way I showed support to my spouse. As a prayer warrior, praying was never a struggle for me. I always made sure my husband was lifted up in my prayers. My prayers were to keep my husband at the foot of the cross, to keep him humble, and to ask God to order his steps as well as keep his ears close to God's mouth so he could hear directly from God. I thought that consistently praying for my husband would suffice. While there is value in prayer, I found out that I needed to do more than just pray for my husband.

I had not realized how critical it was for us to be there for each other. In addition to prayers, what my husband really needed was for me to be there for him physically. As I'm sitting here writing this book, I begin to reminisce on the opportunities that presented itself, but I had made many excuses for why I could not seize them. On several occasions when my husband was traveling to various preaching engagements, I didn't go with him. One specific time that really stood out to me was when my husband had to preach at a women's conference. After having already attended two church services that day, I did not want to go to a third service. I was too tired and drained to travel with my husband to attend this women's gathering. Therefore, I let him go alone.

Another time, my husband was preparing to fly to Africa for an engagement, which was about an 18-hour flight. I also had many explanations as to why I could not attend: the flight was too long, the cost was too high, there was no one to take care of my kids (although my Mother in-law only stayed two blocks from me at that time), etc. Again, I allowed him to go without me.

However, during the time my husband was gone, I had a conversation with one of the elders. She was the mother of our church, Georgia Foster, also known as "Granny." She began to instruct me to never let my husband go anywhere alone. She stated, "Every time your husband travels, you need to be there with him." Prior to that comment, I did not see anything wrong with my actions. I immediately accepted her advice and began to thank God for covering my marriage as the enemy could have come in to destroy my it. I was then reminded of this Scripture:

If you listen to advice and are willing to learn, one day you will be wise.

Proverbs 19:20 GNT

Since then, I always made sure I travel with my Husband everywhere he goes.

Discovering the Truth

My marriage has not always been great. Like most relationships, we had issues that could have torn our union apart if left unresolved. During a time in our marriage, my husband and I were very disconnected. I was doing my own thing, and my husband was doing his own thing. The church was everything to him, the place where he gave it all his attention and energy. My children were everything to me. One day, realizing that were both unhappy, we had a conversation about everything that was going on, and the big "D" word came up, DIVORCE.

This was so devastating to me! But it became a wake-up call for the both of us. This conversation brought clarity to where we were in our marriage. Although we were not doing well, I had not thought that divorce was a factor. Lack of communication could have you think everything is ok when it really is not. We both knew we loved each other and that we wanted to be together. Moreover, prior to our marriage, we vowed that we would never get divorced. A verse in Ecclesiastes played a significant role in this decision:

It is better not to vow than to make a vow and not fulfill it.
Ecclesiastes 5:5 NIV

Our vows were too important to us, so we knew we had to make some adjustments if we wanted our marriage to work.

The first step we made was in starting date nights. This included going to dinner or doing an activity together each week. With that, we set a specific day where we would just spend time together. We made rules for ourselves, like giving each other our full attention during our date nights and putting our phones up as we would spend quality time together. We even made sacrifices that included doing things that we didn't like. For example, my husband liked to go to the movies at least once a week, but I did not like the movies. So, although I used to avoid going to the movies, I would go as a way of showing support since I knew that he enjoyed it. Ironically, I eventually discovered that I really enjoy going to the movies with my spouse. It is not so much about watching a movie, but it is more about the time we spend together.

Similarly, I love shopping, and my spouse does not like it. But my spouse always supports everything that is an interest to me. So, because he knew that I loved to shop, he would go with me. Looking at the bigger picture, it is very important to not get caught up in a task and forget about its purpose. Before, I would not do an activity with my spouse if I did not like it. Now, there is nothing I would not do that includes being around my husband.

POINTS TO PONDER

Always have real conversations with your spouse about his needs or desires. This will show the areas in which you can support him rather than having to assume what his needs are.

If possible, always make yourself available for your spouse's needs. However, this does not mean neglecting yourself.

In addition, always be your spouse's number one supporter. You should not allow anyone to be more supportive of your husband than you are. For example, my husband has always wanted to go fishing, but he did not know how to fish. Because I knew it was something he desired, I would encourage him to get with his friends who are fishermen in order to learn. He received my advice and recently went fishing with his friends. He even caught the biggest fish. I celebrated with him as this was a dream come true for him. I recommend in your quiet time with your spouse, whatever his desires are, that you encourage him to meet his goals.

Baggage can become very heavy if not constantly unloaded. Because of the many issues I faced during my childhood, my marriage was affected. If you have baggage that needs to be resolved, it is so important that you go through a healing process before uniting with your significant other. The key to healing is acknowledgment. If you are honest and acknowledge that you have baggage, then you can get the help that you need. It will ensure you that the baggage that you carry does not become a burden to your partner and that the weight does not hinder you or keep you from moving forward.

Do what you can to support your husband. It is very easy to pay attention to other things that need to be done and neglect the things your spouse needs. I was so focused on what my children needed that I neglected my Husband when he needed me. Pay attention that you are not so focused on things that need to be done and don't see what's not being done.

POINTS TO PRACTICE

Create a vision board and utilize it to keep you on track. To increase support in our marriage, my husband and I created a vision board. On that vision board, we put things that include things we both like, such as trips, dinners, vacations, goals, etc. We placed this vision board in our room, so each time we enter the room, we are able to see and live it.

Always make time for your partner. Because my husband and I did not make time for each other, it almost destroyed our marriage. We realized that, even in our busiest schedules, we must make it a priority to make time for each

other as it is essential to growth in our marriage. In addition, it creates a strong bond between you and your spouse. Be consistent! Make a schedule and stick to it. If it's once a week or twice a month, stick to a day in which you and your spouse can spend time together. Date nights with your spouse do not always have to involve cash. You can do a picnic with your spouse, take a walk to the park, or take a blanket and lay by the beach. This way, you and your spouse will remain connected with each other.

POINTS TO PRAY
Here's my prayer for you, reader:
Lord, I pray for women or men who are reading this book to become closely connected to their spouse through their support. Where there is lack of support, let there be an increase through honest communication.

I encourage you to say this prayer.

Most Gracious Father,

I thank You for everything that You allow me to go through that made me the supportive wife that I am today. Thank You for wisdom and insight on how to be a woman who supports her husband. Thank You Lord for the relationship I have with You that allows me to come to You and cast my cares upon You and receive instructions for my marriage.

As Your Word declares in 1 Peter 5:7, "Casting all your care upon him; for he careth for you" (KJV). Thank You, God, for not allowing my past to ruin my future with my spouse. Lord, help me to become my spouse's number one supporter. Thank you, Lord, for hearing and answering all of my prayers. Isaiah 65:24 says, "Before they call, I will answer; while they are still speaking, I will hear." Lord, help me to be receptive and sensitive to my spouse's needs. In Jesus' Name, Amen.

8
The Darkness Behind the Scenes
Queenie Jean Oakes

I have been married three times. It's hard to believe—I know! It is not something that I am proud of, but my ignorance to the behind-the-scenes spiritual world set me up for my failures. I grew up loving God and following His ways, but when I went to college, I left God and the "good girl" behind. I placed God in my hip pocket and told him "see you later".

In rebellion, I began searching for male attention to meet my needs, often in unhealthy ways, which included smoking pot, partying with liquor, and promiscuity. In the next few pages, I am going to convey the relationships of my life, my mistakes, and the conclusions I have drawn about them. I take full responsibility for my role and do not blame my imperfect husbands as I am imperfect as well.

First Marriage

I was thrilled to be the maid of honor in my best friend's wedding where I met the best man. We began dating, and I fell madly in love with him. He was charming like my dad. I could hardly believe he was actually interested in and attracted to me considering that my own dad hardly knew I existed. He gave me the male attention I had craved all of my life. He was a nice person and a military vet having had life experiences that intrigued me. I was loved and accepted by his family, including his three brothers, while my own brothers ignored me. This also filled gaps in my brokenness.

At the age of 19, I had no idea what I was doing and was giddy with infatuation. I married him after a whirlwind courtship. Because he served in the reserves, there were weekends when he wasn't around. At the time I did not know but this made me feel lonely and abandoned. He was not always there for me, which triggered the wounds from my dad because my dad had not been there for me either. During my husband's absence, I would occasionally have weekend encounters with other men, endeavoring to fulfill my needs outside the marriage just as my Dad had done. I wasn't even aware that I was caught up in a generational curse, and playing it out seemed natural. Although my mother had been angry with my father, she always allowed him to come back to her. This dysfunction blinded me to the possible negative outcomes of my behavior. It didn't dawn on me that my husband could leave me without me feeling abandoned.

It was like the saying: "Looking for love in all the wrong places." Believing the grass was greener on the other side of the fence, I ran from him after only 18 months.

Second Marriage

I had no idea the other side of the fence was a septic tank. Life quickly became messy. A friend was going on vacation to Disneyland in Los Angeles and invited me to join her. I had never flown before and was excited to see the West Coast. We stayed with her family. I met her cousin, and like my Dad, he had good looks and a charismatic personality. He appeared to have his act together, and he had a good job managing a shoe store. He was more than interested in me and invited me to come back to California to live with him.

Again, it was exhilarating and exciting to me that such a good-looking man was interested in me. I left my first husband without much thought about what I was doing. I moved across the country to be with this young man that I hardly knew. I left everything, including my estranged husband, family, friends, and all my possessions, except my clothing. I even left my fabulous job managing the X-Ray Medical Secretary Department in a new hospital. Because I had yet to deal with my own demons, things unknown to me were at play. What was dysfunctional seemed normal.

Impulsively, I moved in with him, which was really against God's law and will for me. It was mostly good for a while. But I eventually began to realize that he was extremely insecure and controlling in our relationship. I felt smothered and trapped by his insecurity. Coupled with my lustful bent, the situation could become explosive. I actually called my first husband in New Jersey, wanting to go back to him. Unlike my mother who always allowed my Dad to return, he said no and that it was over for us the moment I left.

As a result, I decided to stay in California and try to make it work with this new man. In California, I worked jobs in medical administration. Like my mom, I was in denial about how bad our relationship really was or how broken I was, and I always hoped things would get better.

As in the natural progression of the relationship, we married after a few years of being together. It seemed like the thing to do. In about a year or so, I was surprised to find I had been pregnant and suffered a miscarriage. I was fired from my position at work because of malicious attacks by jealous coworkers. It was a very painful time in my life, a pain that seemed unbearable.

The enemy was adding wound after wound, and I felt so helpless. A siren went off as my wakeup call. I knew that God had not caused the bad things to happen. I recognized it was time to get my act together by putting away the foolish things of the world and coming back to God. I repented and wholeheartedly went back to God.

I attended a local church and began the long road to straighten out my relationship with God. It was a great church, and I prospered spiritually. My husband claimed he was an atheist or agnostic, yet the journey of him seeking God for himself followed. On that path, he became a believer, and we attended church together.

After that, we had two beautiful daughters. Like my mother, I resigned from my career to be a stay at home mom. I felt very fulfilled. They were my pride and joy and meant the world to me. Life and relationship between my husband

and me were good for a lot of the time. When it was good, it was great. But when it was bad, it was really bad. It turned out that, like my father, I still had fidelity and relationship issues. Being in church and loving God did not take these things away. Coupled with a depressed man, it was a setup for disaster. We were saved, but we were not delivered; even though we were loving God and attending church, we were not yet free.

He was very much like my father who was controlling and verbally abusive. He wanted me to stay at home and did not want me to have a career. I complied with his demands as I was eager to spend all my time with my children. I was a stay-at-home mom and did all the things to nurture my children, with dance lessons, playing sports, private school tuition, room mother, provided transportation, and attended class trips. All the while, my husband worked 10 to 12 hours a day, 5 days a week and some Saturdays.

My husband wanted to know where I was most of the time, often checking on me during his work day. He finally allowed me to become a part-time beauty consultant with Mary Kay. Even though I was still a full-time, stay-at-home mother, I loved the break from home and my new-found belief in myself. As my self-confidence and self-worth increased, I began being attracted to the attention of other men again. I realized my old nature was alive and well. It had just been hiding, waiting for the best time to come out and cause destruction. We are told to crucify our flesh, not to appease it, but as the men would give me attention, it fed my old needs and old desires. My image changed from housewife to business woman. I gained much respect from my colleagues as I traveled on the road to success earning honors. I received a master's degree in life by growing in Mary Kay.

I met a man at a Friday night happy hour at a local restaurant and lounge. I actually made a secret appointment to meet him for lunch at the beach. Somehow, my husband was suspicious and fearful and confronted me about cheating on him. I had, in fact, stepped out to lunch with another man, and the crap hit the fan. I had deeply hurt my husband. I was very sorry for doing that, but something that was not of God compelled me to go out to lunch. I loved God, yet I had not fully surrendered to God. Moreover, the demons and curses that I had yet to deal with overpowered my desire for God. I needed to be delivered.

My demonic cocktail had me starving for male attention as my husband worked to support the family. This new role of independence and stepping out to lunch set ablaze a crazy situation with my husband. He became increasingly out of control and violent. He put his fists through windows, throw furniture, and terrorized the girls and myself. For example, one Sunday morning as I was getting ready for church, he threw a dust buster through the bathroom window. My youngest daughter became incredibly ridden with anxiety shaking and crying. She was clinging to me and I held her trying to console her. We got prayer after the church service and she received some relief. Something I know now that I did not know then was that demons had entered through open doors on both of our parts. I lived in fear and terror of what he would do next to control me. Hindsight showed me it wasn't control that I needed, but I needed acceptance from my mate as I was constantly under scrutiny for not rising to his demands and expectations.

Fear is not the peace of God, but it is a symptom of the enemy's attack. My husband even controlled a lot of what we ate. He disliked most vegetables, including cooked carrots with pot roast. He thought he was funny and disrespected my desire to feed my family healthy foods. He once took a carrot and put it in his pocket to show the girls his disrespect towards me. This was an ongoing problem at dinner time as I insisted that the girls eat vegetables in keeping with healthy standards. He mocked my efforts, and I believe that his behavior led to one of my daughters having issues with food as she subsequently became anorexic and bulimic.

I recognized I needed help with my emotional issues. I begged him to go to counseling with me, but he refused counseling for himself as he insisted that he didn't need it and that I was the problem. His anger and violence increased so much that the police took him to jail and the mental hospital a few times. When he returned the last time, he even cursed me by saying, "If you think the girls are mad at you now, wait until they don't want anything to do with you." He also told me that he would "take me down" financially. I had no idea that it was truly his intention. He later realized that he really needed counselling, so he decided to go and has continued to do so since that time, as far as I know.

The stress was unbearable, living in constant fear, guilt, and shame. I begged him to leave the home for a separation in order for me to have time to receive counsel. He vehemently refused, and it left me no choice but to find a place to be safe. I left home with the girls as I was their caregiver and was consumed with fear of his rage. Because of the kindness of my church leaders, I stayed in a home that harbored victims. After a short time of counseling, hiding, and separation, the girls and I returned to our home, much too soon.

I wanted to reconcile, work out our differences, and save our marriage, but reconciliation was not on his mind. He used this time to alienate our daughters from me. In the end, just like he had predicted, I lost everything, including my children. I did not want my children separated from each other, so I was bullied into agreeing that they stay in the family home with him while I had 30 percent visitation, and if they did not want to come visit, they did not have to come. He made a lot of promises about reducing his work hours, learning to cook, transport them to school, and many other things. I wanted the girls to stay together, not splitting them apart, keep them in the same school system and maintain some stability. I let the girls live with their father. My mistake was believing his promises.

I was so emotionally devastated that I could not maintain my business as a director in Mary Kay, and I had to relinquish my position, my free company car, and my home. I divorced him because I was weakened and emotionally bankrupt. It seemed as if there was no way to fix this damaged relationship. My mother always said she married for life, no matter what my father did. I followed in her footsteps until there was nothing left to give.

The girls had a deep disrespect for me at this point. I was guilt driven, wounded, and damaged and I went through a lot of counseling. The girls were in a tumultuous situation, and their suffering anguished me. When her father could not control our oldest daughter any longer, he threw her out and she moved in with me. The girls were now split up, breaking my heart.

Third Marriage

Within a few years, I believed I had gotten over the emotional turmoil and thought I was ready for a new male relationship, but I wasn't fully healed or truly delivered.

I met John on a bike path at the beach. He was an avid cyclist, and we both attended the same church. We were buddies, pals, and then became best friends. I tried to fix him up with my friends, but one of them finally said, "He is *your* friend; you date him." I started to see John as more than just a friend after her comments. John was unlike my first two husbands. He was gentle, we talked for hours, and we were great companions. He was stable and had a long-standing career. We took dance lessons together.

We fell in love. This time, I was determined to have God's best by doing it His way. In preparation for our marriage, we read the book, *Preventing Divorce* by Greg and Candy McPherson and Bob and Cheryl Biehl, and we thoughtfully answered the assigned questions in the book.

We had our wedding overlooking the Pacific Ocean at sunset. It had been raining all day, but it stopped just in time for our ceremony. It was absolutely beautiful. Both of my daughters were in the wedding with us, and that was delightful. It was like a breath of fresh air came upon my life that day. We were very peaceful, and our relationship was in harmony. Fast forward. We have just celebrated 21 years of marriage. It has not always been easy, but we have committed our lives to God and to each other. In the beginning years, we started three home groups sponsored by our church leadership. It was a highlight of our lives, building others while strengthening our faith and union with God.

John's career came to a screeching halt in a few years. This eliminated his security in his work. He found several contract jobs, and the jobs finally concluded. This was really hard on him psychologically and emotionally. He struggled with depression and self-worth, and I tried to comfort his pain in response. Unfortunately, he was spiraling down the emotional path. It caused marital issues that we were not prepared to handle.

John and I moved to Phoenix and became a part of a large ministry. After that, we helped a woman from South Africa start a local church. Even though we were both wholeheartedly seeking God, we still had life issues, including curses and demonic oppression in our lives. It was during this period of time that we began to understand the need for soul restoration, which included demonic deliverance.

We both encountered generational family curses, including anger, adultery, rejection, abandonment, lust, and abuse. I came to realize many of my bad behaviors were because of these curses that I knew nothing about. Slowly, we began the deliverance process, and God healed us from these unclean spirits. They were removed from the recesses of our souls. God gave us a hunger to help others in the same way that we had been set free. We had much training all over the U.S. and started a ministry of healing and deliverance for others. Our heart's desire is that both sides of our entire family lines be healed. Healing is a process and a painful journey that includes looking at our past, looking at our present, and looking forward towards a better future. It is well worth the effort it takes to get to the side of freedom.

Before, my marriages were demonically driven and so are many other marriages. When we don't know what is operating, we don't know how to fight and therefore diminish our chances to win!

Throughout our marriage, my husband and I have worked really hard to keep it moving forward. This has not been an easy path for either one of us. I believe we are experiencing a successful marriage. The continuous effort to be united has allowed us to conquer our past. We have learned that compromise on both of our parts in order to seek solutions to the issues in life has produced great rewards. It is only because of our faith in God that He has blessed our efforts. It is only because of God that we stand firm in our resolve to keep going. God has continued to unite us in order for His will to be done in our lives.

Where I Went Wrong

As a young woman beginning college, I should have been determined to stay close to God. When I put Him in my back pocket and said, "See you later," it opened the door to partying, evil, and doing wrong things.

I could have "stuck it out" with my first husband as I did love him. His family was warm and welcoming. I am still friends with all of his siblings to this day. He was a nice guy, but I wasn't ready for marriage, and I should not have married him. I was far too young and immature.

I should not have been so eager to go with the second guy on an impulsive whim. I had a good career with a good future, and an estranged husband. I threw it all away to be with a man I didn't really know. If I had taken the time to know him before committing to a live-in relationship, I would have seen the warning signs of his instability.

Even with my third husband, I was not healed, so I brought that hurt into our marriage. He has been kind, but it would've been much better if I had been healed prior to marrying him.

Out of the neglect of my relationship with God, I failed to recognize my calling in life.

The thief does not come except to steal, and to kill, and to destroy.
John 10:10, NKJV

Through family curses, he nearly destroyed me.

POINTS TO PONDER
Avoid the Potholes.

Keep your eyes on Jesus, maintaining your relationship with Jesus and discerning His will. Just going to church is not the answer. So many can go to church and never really know Him.

Do not ignore your inner conscience, which is from God.

Not only know who you are, but know whose you are!

Slow down and seek God's guidance. Impulsiveness can lead to a bitter path of destruction as I personally experienced.

Experience your need for love through Jesus, not people, or church. It is the highest love that no human can provide, not even husbands, parents, and children. Know that others cannot give you what they do not have to give.

POINTS TO PRACTICE
Read and answer the questions from the book that I mentioned earlier, *Preventing Divorce*. So many pitfalls in your relationship can be avoided when you seriously embrace and take action with this book. It was so helpful to John and I prior to our marriage that we consider it an indispensable tool for those pursuing the possibilities of marriage.

Do not become physically intimate until the ink is dried on the marriage certificate.

Counseling is no substitute for deliverance. Demons must be cast out and not medicated or counseled.

Marriage is a covenant between three; God, husband, and wife. Seek God first, and then seek your spouse.

You must have an attitude of compromise and yield yourself to God and your mate.

Do not be a "right fighter." It doesn't matter who is right and who is wrong. We must be in tune with God and his desires for unity.

Desire to serve one another. Marriage is not 50/50. At all times, we must give 100% and not expect a 50/50 deal. Many a marriage will fail with the expectation for everything to be equal.

- Pray separately and together.
- Read the Word separately and together.
- Seek wise counsel from mature married folks.
- Repent quickly.
- Avoid self-accusation.
- Do not marry someone who is not equally yoked spiritually.
- Forgive yourself and others.
- Continue to enable yourself to believe that God has forgiven you and is not mad at you.

POINTS TO PRAY

Heavenly Father, I bless Your holy name. I thank You for creating marriage. I thank You that You are an all-forgiving God and that without You, I am nothing. I pray for the power of Your Holy Spirit to inhabit each of the people who read this. I ask that they will seek Your will for their spouse or future spouse and that they listen to Your still, small voice. May Your Spirit be poured out and lead all into paths of righteousness.

The spirit of the LORD is upon Me, because the LORD has anointed Me to preach good tidings to the poor; He has sent Me to heal the broken hearted, To proclaim liberty to the captives, And the opening of the prison to those who are bound.

Isaiah 61:1 NKJV

9
It's Me, It's Me, It's Me, Oh Lord
Katherine Gamble

It all began before we were married. She was coming! My love's eight-year-old daughter was coming from Virginia for a visit. I was excited that my new love would have the opportunity to spend time with his little girl. At the same time, I began to feel anxious because I didn't know what to expect. I wasn't sure how I would receive her or vice versa. Though my love and I weren't married, I was his "baby," and he treated me as such. He treated me like I was very special and demonstrated love, affection, and attention to me in a way that I'd never before received it. I didn't want to lose or jeopardize this love. I allowed my emotions to consume me. I became frustrated and very overwhelmed.

The day she arrived, everything seemed normal. All the emotions I previously felt appeared to be gone or, at least I thought they were. The next morning, there was already a difference. When I woke up, he was gone, certainly not his normal routine. I tried to control my emotions because I immediately started feeling angry. I was usually the one who wakes up and prepares breakfast for the family, so why did he get up that day?

At first, I didn't say anything to him. I waited for a little while and then got up to see what he was doing. He had made breakfast and was cutting up his daughter's food as if she was five years old. I became livid. All I could think about was how when I met him, my youngest son was eight years old, and he didn't get up early and prepare breakfast for my son. I started an ugly argument with him and became so upset that I threw a plate of food against the kitchen wall. I just didn't care and wanted to give up on all of it.

The next morning, his daughter approached the bedroom's open doorway, and she greeted him with a cheerful, "Good morning, Daddy." Then she left to watch television. I was so upset. She didn't address me at all. I reasoned that maybe she wasn't sure what to call me, so I decided not to say anything at all. When I mentioned it to her dad, he told her to call me mom.

I didn't feel comfortable with that because we were not married yet. I thought maybe she could call me Ms. Katherine. For the entire three weeks, she did not address me by anything other than "ummm." That isn't even a word. I was addressed by a sound. I felt so unappreciated. I had been with her father for two years, and I had sent her gifts the entire time. Perhaps her mom never told her, but that didn't matter to me. I felt I had a valid reason to disengage. I wanted to give up on building a relationship before I ever really gave it a try. "Petty Patty" was in full effect!

After her stay was over and she had returned home, I consistently argued with him about every little thing. I was literally being petty. I had become the problem, and I had no solution on how to overcome the behavior I was projecting towards others in the home. I began to feel rejected, something I was very familiar with. I wondered if this relationship was meant to be, and if so, I wondered how I would get past the emotions. I began to pray about the situation and solicited prayer from others who I knew pray for me concerning the difficult situation.

Shortly afterwards, my love and I were married. Remember, I had been with him for two years, and by now, I thought I should be delivered from all of those horrible emotions. Well, year after year, his daughter would come for the summer or for spring break, and I would realize that I still wasn't over this mountain. The fact that her visit always took place a few days before our anniversary made me even more furious. I had arranged for my kids to be with their grandmother so that my husband and I could have some special time together. I didn't want anything to interfere with the plans we had made, and that included having to find a babysitter for his daughter.

I eventually began to see why my behavior was childish. It was then that I asked GOD to reveal the root of this problem to me. I knew beyond a shadow of a doubt that it was deeper than what I could see or perceive. GOD began to reveal so much to me *about me*. There was an issue, and GOD said to me, "The issue IS YOU, Katherine." Woah—talk about a hard pill for me to swallow. At that point, I was in denial for sure.

I wondered how I could overcome this obstacle that seemed to fester more and more. I began to read the Bible a little more intimately. There was a Scripture that captured my attention and heart:

Study and be eager and do your utmost to present yourself to God approved (tested by trial), a workman who has no cause to be ashamed, correctly analyzing and accurately dividing [rightly handling and skillfully teaching] the Word of Truth.
2 Timothy 2:15 AMPC

I was led to study and show myself approved by rightly dividing the Word of Truth into my own

I was being tested by trial as a workman of GOD and needed not to be ashamed.

I had another favorite Scripture:

You will guard him and keep him in perfect and constant peace whose mind [both its inclination and its character] is stayed on You, because he commits himself to You, leans on You, and hopes confidently in You.

Isaiah 26:3 AMPC

Isaiah 26:3 became my shield, and GOD kept me in perfect peace as I kept my mind on Him. I started to invest in myself for personal and spiritual growth. I attended a weekly women's meeting at my church and participated in the activities in order to be more engaged. I volunteered more in my Church and began to see myself maturing in the things of GOD. This alone helped me spiritually and emotionally, and I began to identify the real issue. I needed to make a change and do it quickly because I was hurting my marriage and family.

Everyone in my home could feel my negative emotions. I really felt awful and needed GOD to answer me or send help to assist me with this dilemma. Daily, I would examine my heart to see what I needed to change. Over and over, I only came up against what I felt was a wall. I was really stuck between a rock and a hard place in my life and couldn't find freedom. I began to realize that the little girl in me was resisting the opportunity to forgive and get past the rejection that I had experienced for too long. I had grown accustomed to being the only female in the house and never had to address it before she came to visit because it was never presented until now. God exposed the area in which I finally needed to be delivered, but I was too stubborn to accept the deliverance that He freely offered. I felt no one understood me.

I justified my position because I had to be independent. This was a result of my mom putting me out of her house at the age of 18. This also made me a little possessive though I didn't know it. Everything was "my this" or "my that." I pretty much controlled the flow of things in my home, the home that I had purchased eight years prior. I certainly didn't mean any harm.

However, I recognized that my husband would become really upset whenever I used the word "my." I could not understand what the big deal was. "Here we go again," I would think, "Something else wrong with me." I didn't know what I was going to do, but I was ready to live a drama free life.

Enough was enough. I prayed for HOLY SPIRIT to help me because I did not know how to change what I didn't think was wrong. I continued with "my car," "my phone," "my room," "my kitchen," "my door," "my," "my," "my..." I was told that I wanted to wear the skirt *and* the pants in the relationship. I heard these words quite often, more than I wanted to. I refused to see that something was wrong, and I argued without ceasing.

Finally, I decided to humble myself and allow GOD to work on me. I embraced this Scripture in Colossians:

Be gentle and for bearing with one another and, if one has a difference (a grievance or complaint) against another, readily pardoning each other; even as the Lord has [freely] forgiven you, so must you also [forgive].

Colossians 3:13, AMPC

This required us to bear with each other and forgive whatever grievances we had towards one another, just as GOD had forgiven us. Even though I STILL didn't see where I was wrong, I wanted to have peace and reconciliation with my husband. Instead of trying to point a finger at him, I allowed GOD to reveal my inner me to me, and things began to change in my favor.

I purposefully paid close attention to the words that I was speaking, and I spoke a little slower. Actually, I had to think before I spoke as taught in elementary school and in the Scriptures. Boy, did the atmosphere around me begin to shift in a positive direction. There were times when I would revert back to "my this" or "my that," not intentionally, but quickly in order to apologize and make up. I would not allow such a petty issue to cause division between us.

Now we are married, and it's our third year in this relationship. Just when you think you know your spouse, things you didn't know him begin to surface. You come to realize that he still doesn't like certain things you say and do, and you notice that you don't like a lot of his habits either. Arguments begin to arise out of nowhere, arising from so many little things. For example, your spouse may complain and begin to ask, "Why do you wash your hands in the kitchen sink?" or "Why do you shake your hands dry over the tiled floor and not use a paper towel?" or "Why do you spit in the bedroom trash that we both use?" "Why, why, why..."

I was not sure why these questions that had never been important before suddenly agitated him so much. I gave my husband such a hard time. I began to pray, and I resumed seeking GOD concerning myself. What was my problem? I absolutely did not know, but I was determined to resolve this issue because I needed to be happy.

As it turned out, I was the root of my unhappiness. After speaking with a few sisters in my church's women's meeting, I realized that the problem could very well be me. Apostle Idella once told us that this type of control could be a form of witchcraft. Well, I certainly was not a witch and did not want any of the characteristics of a witch. I read the Scriptures and connected with the Word that talked about GOD not giving us the spirit of fear, but of love, power, and a sound mind/self-discipline or self-control. The only area in which I needed to have control over was myself, and I had not mastered that. I did some self-reflection and really practiced new habits that forced me to change from the control freak that I had allowed life to make me.

At first, it was extremely hard. I was so used to having things a certain way and doing things my own way that I felt myself resisting the change that was so necessary for my love with my husband to be nurtured and strengthened even more. The Scripture about how a husband would rather live on a rooftop than with a bickering woman really convicted me. Another verse refers to a bickering woman as a raindrop continually falling on a tin roof. Wow, every time I opened the Bible, and I opened it quite often, I would be convicted. I would think, "What about him? He is not perfect," but HOLY SPIRIT continued to reveal things to me about myself because I was the one being pruned and prepared.

With marriage, there are many topics that one must discuss. I found myself asking, "Is this blended family stuff really worth it?" My three sons were sort of out of control as they entered their preteen years. My husband only had one-daughter who was totally different from my sons, so I could not figure out how to get him to understand my sons or my parenting strategies. I disciplined my sons since they were toddlers, and they definitely knew that I did not play. They continued to do any and everything to rebel against what they had been taught. My marriage was in jeopardy once again. I was a good mother, and my sons being disrespectful to me was not acceptable to my husband. I understood the logic behind his point of view, but I didn't see it as a reason for us to end the marriage.

We know how the devil works. He likes to use situations to magnify differences. I recall a time when we had a disagreement in the relationship and could not come to an understanding on how to move forward. I believed that this was unfair. I became upset and a little resentful at this point.

I allowed these emotions to affect my relationship with my stepdaughter. I knew that I was not going to treat her any different from how I treated my sons. Although some of my sons had been in trouble in school and even placed in juvenile detention, they were still my young children. I refused to give up on them or put them on the street. This put a strain on my marriage, and we almost let it go. The Bible lets us know that love covers a multitude of sins, and that is for sure. Love kept our marriage and family when we had checked out.

I believe because we gave our marriage to GOD from the beginning in spirit and in truth, He was always the center and has kept us together. When we were first married, we lifted our marriage up before GOD and gave it to Him. Starting in 2007, we began every morning, and we have continued this for over seven years faithfully. At first, I would lead the prayers, but I eventually decided it was time for him to do so because he was the head of the house. I even typed a prayer that included a few Scriptures. My husband and I would get on our knees and pray at approximately 5:30am each morning. Soon after, we invited our two sons in to pray before their school day. Having the boys included became a distraction after a few months, and we later excused the boys. For years, we never stopped praying together, and by faith, we knew that was the reason we could have our disagreements, forgive, and move on. I truly believe that prayer changes things, and a family that prays together gains the strength to remain together through trials and tribulations.

Just when it seemed like things were finally coming to an end with all the chaos, confusion, and disarray, my youngest son decided to use drugs at age seventeen. This must have been the most difficult time of my life. No one could seem to understand the spiritual warfare that I was battling on a daily basis, and that made it extremely frustrating. I had been with my husband since this child was eight years old. It was hard to process that my son was now dealing with mental health issues due to drug usage. I was constantly reminded of Scriptures by HOLY SPIRIT. One particular Scripture that helped me to keep focus was found in Proverbs:

Train up a child in the way he should go: and when he is old, he will not depart from it.

Proverbs 22:6 KJV

I was faithful in raising my kids up in the LORD with good morals and values. That Scripture gave me hope.

This experience brought much heartache and pain to all parties involved, mostly to my son, my husband, and to me. During the three years, on many occasions, we talked about just throwing in the towel and going our separate ways. I continued to trust my marriage vows and held onto the fact that what GOD has joined together, let no man—and that included me—put asunder.

My husband was on the ledge about the entire situation. My prayers kept both of us holding on. Though he didn't want a divorce, he continued to say over and over that we should live separately. I refused to come into agreement with something that I knew GOD had not spoken.

Every day, my son seemed to be getting worse and not better. There were many prayer warriors praying on our behalf, but it seemed that I was all alone and that the situation was hopeless. I had taken my son from counselor to counselor and to one hospital after another with no resolve. He had been Baker acted on seven occasions in one year. I had exhausted all my options and was really stuck between a rock and a hard place. I literally stopped talking to people about what was going on and focused solely on the WORD of GOD. I prayed without ceasing and purposefully got up each morning as much as possible to spend time in the presence of GOD alone. I needed to hear from GOD desperately. As soon as I stopped trying to fix everything in my own strength, I began to see the hand of GOD move.

The hospital that we were going to for medication offered a program through which a counselor would travel to our home every week and visit with my son. This was the breakthrough that our family needed. The male counselor was able to communicate with my son, and that opened doors to receive the help that no one had been able to give him. My son was distant and not speaking much during all of this, but now he is speaking again. His thoughts began to come together for him once again, and he can communicate with others around him. At this point, he was able to do a lot more for himself since he felt safe to open up and share with someone. Everything began to transpire really quickly as his situation had shifted in a positive way. I could see the hand of GOD moving from the north, south, east, and west. My heart began to feel GOD's love again, and I believe that my son, husband, and everyone around could feel the change that had come over me. The release that I had prayed for, cried about, and hoped for was now upon me, the joy that I felt was unspeakable. I prayed for GOD to rekindle the fire that once burned in our marriage, and I began to see change instantly.

What I expect someone to take away from my story is the following: What my anger, anxiety, frustration, and insecurities were really trying to tell me had absolutely nothing to do with normal stepmom stress. I disengaged before giving it an opportunity. I felt unappreciated. I became a very unhealthy individual, physically, emotionally, and spiritually.

POINTS TO PONDER
Do we allow the marriage vows to become null and void when life happens?

When life takes on an emotional roller coaster, is the foundation built strong enough to sustain the marriage?

POINTS TO PRACTICE
Lean not unto our own understanding and perception.

Seek help and guidance from trusted and credible resources.

Keep the lines of communication open in the relationship. Focus on changing yourself instead of pointing the blame on others.

POINTS TO PRAY
Pray to get an understanding of the root of the problem.

Pray for deliverance in the area of offense.

Pray to forgive quickly, and give others the freedom to change.
Abba Father, GOD, I thank you for teaching me to get an understanding concerning the root of a matter. I seek deliverance in every area of offense. I allow myself space to increase in your wisdom pertaining to family matters. Let me

always forgive quickly and release others so that they may also show forgiveness. Help me, LORD, to allow others the freedom to change in your perfect timing. In the matchless name of JESUS CHRIST, the LORD. Amen.

ABOUT THE AUTHORS

IDELLA LISELLE

Idella Liselle is very unconventional. She looks for opportunities to display GOD's love and power in creative and unique ways. She is radical and out of the box. Her encounters with the LORD are so real and tangible that any other way of living is simply not an option.

She entered into ministry at a young age with a desire to impact her community from the age of 12 until she graduated as Valedictorian at the age of 16. She volunteered four hours each week. This desire for community development from a holistic standpoint continues to spur her outreach efforts even today.

Though single, GOD has used her to restore and reconcile countless marriages. Her wisdom is divine. She promotes sexual integrity as a viable option. She freely shares her testimony of being delivered from sexual perversion and how she is a virgin to this day. She wanted to ensure that, unlike what was available to her, when people want to be free from sexual perversion, they have a place to go to. She has spoken on many platforms against sexual perversion and for the pursuit of holiness.

With over 25 years of walking in the prophetic and 20 years of ministry experience, GOD called Idella to pastor in January 2011. On October 29, 2012, Pastor

Idella heard GOD audibly calling her to the role of Apostle. She is daily growing and maturing in her current assignment.

Since 2009, she has trained countless people on how to hear and recognize GOD's Voice. Idella has a no-nonsense approach to hearing from GOD. She is adamant about keeping it simple. Idella brings further clarity to the prophetic, saying, "not every Christian is a prophet, but every Christian can prophesy." Under R.E.A.L. Ministries Institute, she equips men and women of GOD with tools for ministry and/or ordination.

She serves as Lead Pastor of REAL Ministries Online, C.E.O. Coach and CEO of several other enterprising endeavors, including Kairo Coaching Institute and Publish*her* Publishing

Contact Information

idellaliselle@gmail.com
www.REALMinistries.Online
www.idellalliselle.com
www.publishher.org

FB Info: IdellaLiselle
Instagram: IdellaLiselle
770-727-1669

DEBBIE JONES

Debbie Jones is a teacher who has taught hundreds of children how to read. She has lived on an exotic island, survived Hurricane Matthew, and experienced the wonder of Niagara Falls.

She has also been a switchboard operator, a professional tutor, a teacher, a mentor, and a math interventionist. When she is not reading or writing about marital relationships, she is most likely volunteering at her church in the nursery, vacation bible school, and prayer ministry.

Debbie lives in Jacksonville, Florida with her fun-loving family. She is the wife of a financial analyst and short film writer and the mother of two creative teenagers. Wife Material is her first published book compilation.

CONTACT INFO:
Bornblessed15547@gmail.com

FB: Debbie Jones

MYRLENE WARREN

Myrlene Warren is a Haitian American author. She was born in Haiti but came to the Sunshine State at the age of 12.

After spending much of her career in the social service field, working with children, adults, and the elderly, she was inspired to follow her passion as a writer.

When she is not writing, she enjoys spending time and traveling the world with her family.

Myrlene finds joy in motivating, encouraging, and empowering her audience, which is the goal of her next book titled, *Finding Your Strengths in the Struggles*. For more information on the next book release date, please contact her via the email address provided below.

She currently lives in Orlando Florida with her three children and loving husband whom she's been married to for 6 years.

CONTACT INFO:

AuthorMyrleneWarren@gmail.com

PASTOR ORIENTHIA SPEAKMAN

Pastor Orienthia Speakman is a native of Atlanta, Georgia and is a woman to be emulated. Bold, fierce, explosive, passionate, loved and all about her Father's business!

These are just a few words to describe Pastor Orienthia (also called Pastor "O"). She's the "Keep It Real Preacher" who is not afraid to expose the sinful proclivities plaguing the Body of Christ. Her ministry is on the uprise because of her transparency about her life, issues, and the deliverance she has experienced. Doors have been opened for her to travel around the US, radically changing the lives she encounters. She loves imparting words of wisdom, knowledge, and revelation into the hearts of God's people. Her messages are powerful, impactful, and unforgettable.

Orienthia has a heart for building, equipping and pouring into the hearts of women from all around the world. She's the Founder and CEO of Speak O Worldwide, which is a global mentorship hub for women that focuses on empowering and encouraging sisters through practical biblical teaching to live a balanced and productive, Christ-centered life after they have experienced divorce, becoming a widow, or are simply broken and stagnate due to unexpected circumstances. She empowers them to know that there is a purpose in the process. Giving up is not an option! Pastor Orienthia intentionally ignites a fire that may have been quenched through past hurts, pains, and disappointments by helping women to have "now faith" for "now opportunities" that will produce new beginnings in their lives.

She has been an Ordained Minister since 2000 and has earned a degree in Psychology. Most recently, she has become a Certified Transformational Coach through the International Coaching Federation. Orienthia currently serves as Pastor of Christian Education at Bethel Original Freewill Baptist Church in Decatur, Georgia. Combining her education with the anointing, Orienthia strives to help produce fruit that will last in the lives of God's people. She eagerly imparts the Word of God in such a way that brings illumination and transformation, even to the simplest minds.

She has authored several books: *Really God?: A Guide to Bouncing Back When Life Has Thrown You Down*, *Bouncing Back: A 40-Day Personal Devotional*, *Kingdom Bombshells Guide to being Explosive* (Compilation), and excerpts in, *100 Ways to Be Fabulous Inside and Out*. Her latest releases are *Marriage Vs. Ministry: The Fight of My Life*, and *In the Ring: 31-Day Devotional for Couples*.

Orienthia and her husband Vincent reside in Stone Mountain, Georgia along with their family.
Contact Information:
www.speakorienthia.com
Fb Contacts: Orienthia Speakman
              Speak O
              Butterfly University

IG Contact: pastorospeaks

DR. SAKEISHA HYLICK

Eric & Dr. Sakeisha Hylick are Co-Founders of **Ultimately Y.O.U.**, **Relationship Strategists**, and **Certified Life Coaches.** They have been helping to **Educate, Empower, and Encourage** husbands and wives on how to **WIN** in their marriage. Together, they travel across the United States helping couples to overcome what they refer to as **"The Great Divide"** in marriage. This great divide encompasses challenges in **communication, finances and sex**.

Minister Eric and Dr. Sakeisha are frequently called upon because of their innate ability to help their clients achieve breakthroughs in their relationship struggles. Whether you are experiencing challenges in your relationships spiritually, emotionally, and/or financially, the Hylicks deliver proven systems to break unproductive behavioral patterns and create lifelong change.

This anointed couple demonstrates firsthand what it means to **rebuild trust**, **overcome obstacles**, **bounce back from bankruptcy,** and **focus on forgiveness** while in the midst of **balancing business, family, faith, and finances.** Together, they co-authored a book, **Marriage Can Win**, which is a transparent journey into their quest to remain victorious during the most challenging times in their marriage.

The Hylicks have been featured guest speakers and conference hosts throughout the Southeast Regions of the U.S. to the West Coast and in Hawaii. They are extremely passionate about seeing couples **"thrive"** in their marriages and not **"just survive!"** **Together, the couple hosts group seminars and retreats as well as marriage and relationship workshops.**

This "dynamic duo" has served as co-facilitators in the marriage ministry at their home church. They have been active participants in The Healing Rooms and instructors in the **Bible Institute**. Additionally, they are the co-Founders of **Covenant Kingdom Builders**, an online ministry. This diligent, devoted couple currently resides in **Windermere, Florida** with their two teenage children. You can visit them online at www.marriagescanwin.com.

CONTACT INFO:

FB/TWITTER/INSTAGRAM/YOUTUBE: MARRIAGECANWIN

407-476-8945

PASTOR CAROL SIMPSON

At a young age, God called Pastor Carol Simpson. The hand of God continues to shape her course and destiny as she touches the lives of people. She has been mandated to challenge the Body of Christ to walk in truth, integrity, and CHARACTER.

Pastor Carol has been in ministry for over 30 years and has imparted the Word of God in conferences, seminars and retreats. Her passion is to see the people of God come into maturity; therefore, she has given herself to training, counseling and mentoring for the success of others.

Pastor Carol wrote a monthly article in a magazine The Gospel Times titled, "The Prophetess Corner" where she encouraged Leaders with a Prophetic word and enlightenment. The magazine was a spinoff to a powerful interview Pastor Carol gave entitled, "Church Hurt". Many leaders around the world were also featured in this interview as well.

She has been married to the wonderful Pastor. Nicholas C. Simpson Sr. for over 34 years together they have 3 children and 5 grandchildren. After being employed and licensed in the financial field for over 15 years, God called Pastor Carol into a full-time commitment in ministry.

She is the Founder/Visionary of Women of Integrity Ministries now for over 25 years. She is a Mentor and has 35+ Mentees and hosts a Mentor/Mentee Leadership conference every year in Las Vegas. Her main assignment is pastoring with her husband Pastor Nicholas at Shekinah Glory Ministries.

The Prophetic gift that is upon her is driven by love and based upon the truth of God's word.

CONTACT:

kweensimp2@aol.com

FB: Carol Simpson

Instagram: Rev. Carol Simpson

702-400-9080

ELOIS WASH

Elois Wash is a Christian Author, who is well known for having a great heart for her community. She was born and raised in Orlando, FL, but she moved to Cocoa, FL several years ago where she pastors a church with her husband to whom she has been married for 22 years.

Before becoming a writer, she has had the opportunity to do various ministries with her husband over the years, including marriage ministries, where she learned marriages were suffering. She became a part of this book to be a voice to those who are struggling in their marriage.

When she is not writing, she enjoys shopping and traveling with her husband. Her next book titled, *I'm Walking In My Heeling* will come out in July 2020.

CONTACT:

AuthorEloisWash@gmail.com

QUEENIE JEAN OAKES

Queenie, born Jean Wilkinson, was raised in South Jersey. Queenie is sincere, warm-hearted, and discerning. She sees the best in people and treasures her friends and family.

Queenie loves life and people and truly rejoices when she sees them healed, delivered, and released into their destinies. Serving others comes naturally to her. She is a woman of great faith and is a prophetic evangelist. Queenie is firmly grounded in the Word of God and follows the leading of the Holy Spirit. She connects easily with people, warmly reaching out to others whether in the supermarket or on the Las Vegas strip.

She has over 20 years of medical administrator experience. Her well-known ability to socialize and communicate along with her leadership skills aided her well in her transition to Mary Kay Cosmetics. She worked for 27 years, gaining a Master's Degree in Life. She has also held real estate licenses in two states.

Most recently, Queenie's health required a major overhaul. In her search for health, God led her to a health and wellness company, and she is making remarkable progress. She praises God for a new lease on life and renewed health.

Queenie has been married to John for over 21 years. They knew from the beginning of their marriage that they were to minister together. In Southern California, they lead many home groups. Queenie and John are known as sojourners, following and serving God as He moves them from one place to another. They are pastors and co-founders of Liberated Hearts, a healing and deliverance ministry, and they currently reside in Florida.

CONTACT:

queenjean52@gmail.com

KATHERINE GAMBLE

Katherine is committed to having a great marriage and being the best mother and grandmother. She finds pleasure in sharing how she has been able to overcome many challenges with the help of GOD by leading of the HOLY SPIRIT. She believes some of life's experiences can be gained/learned from someone else's experience instead of enduring the aches and pains from personal experience. Katherine has had the privilege of being mentored by some of the strongest, most spiritual, and wise men and women in the LORD'S army. Her purpose of writing is to enlighten others of the fact that there is always a way of escape and that having patience, persistence, and consistency will always bring out the best in any situation.

She's also been a prayer intercessor and leader of Evangelism. Before she decided to begin writing, she often wrote encouraging quotes to friends and family. She finds it best to write between 3AM and 5AM in her bathroom or in her garage while sitting in the car. She's a sucker for good family relationships and being in love. Katherine gets excited anytime there's kissing, much to the embarrassment of her children. Her husband doesn't seem to complain, however. When she isn't cleaning, cooking, taking care of her granddaughter, or reading, she's probably singing or listening to praise and worship music, watching

Lifetime movies, or watching Netflix movies based on true stories.

Katherine Gamble is a Loan Servicing Representative for Marriott World Wide. Her passion for helping people in all aspects of life flows through life challenges that she has experienced and overcome. She has always loved to write and has encouraged many others by sharing her experiences. She's the wife of a marine veteran, a mother of four young adults, and a grandmother of two grandchildren.

CONTACT INFO

FB: LADYKATHERINE GAMBLE

BECOME AN AUTHOR

Publish*her* is looking for authors for its next compilation.

Has challenges made your life interesting? Do you have a story to tell? Would you like to be an author in our next compilation or have a book you need assistance in publishing? We would love to bring your story to life. Contact us today!

For more information, go to www.publishher.org.

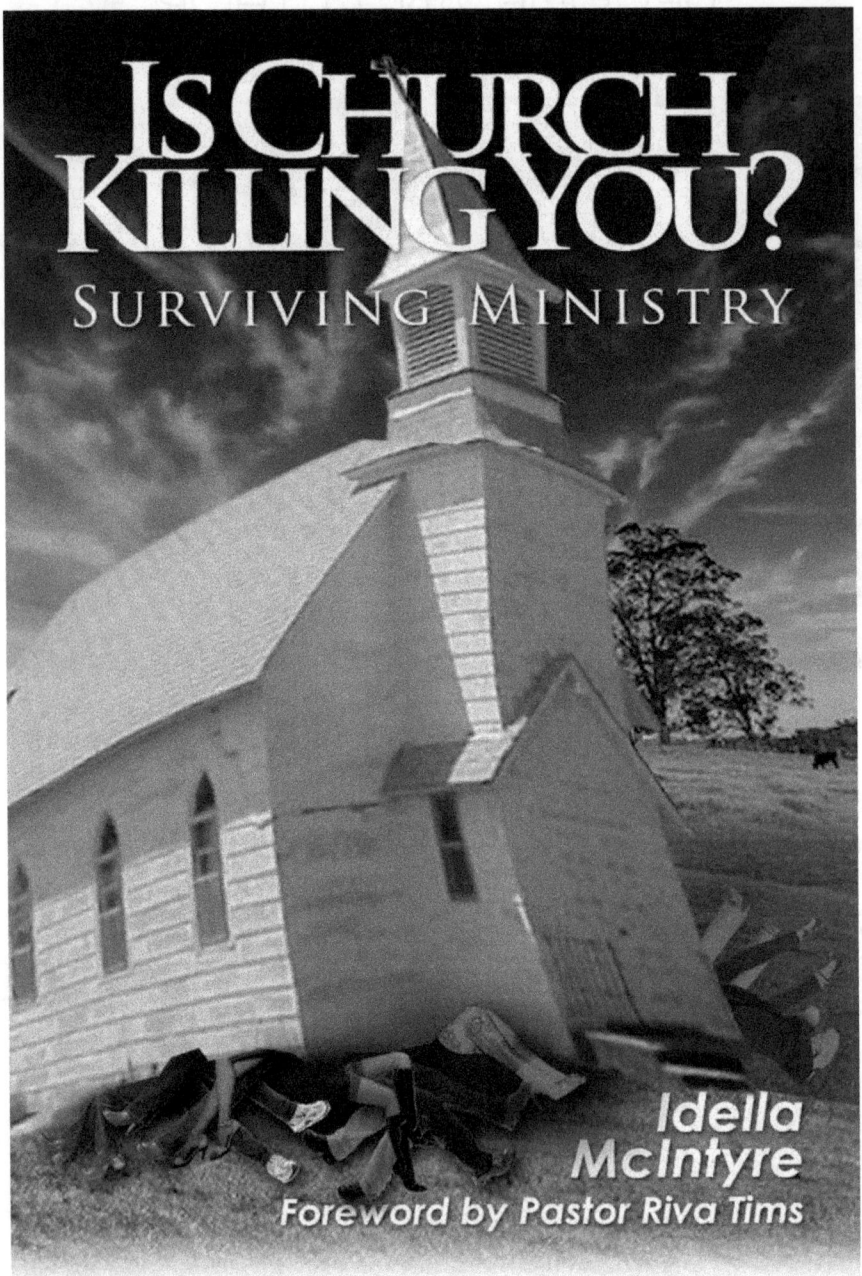

Is Church Killing You? Surviving Ministry Book Excerpt

Deception can only be effectively played on the stage of life if you have the leading role.

The Art of Deception

"And He said, Go and tell this people, Hear ye indeed but understand not; and see ye indeed, but perceive not. Make the heart of this people fat, and make their ears heavy, and shut their eyes; lest they see with their eyes; lest they hear with their ears, and understand with their heart and convert and be healed." **Isaiah 6:9-10(KJV)**

Whenever you identify church hurt, there is a connecting thread of deception. In my experience with church hurt, I saw deception of man, which opened my eyes to the other deception around me and an even greater deception within me.

My encounter with deception brought amazing discoveries. I was determined to never be deceived again. I even purchased a book called, *Never Be Lied to Again*. I was challenged to know what was real from what was Memorex. What was the church that GOD wanted me to experience, and what was the church that I had created through opinions and excuses of man?

I was being inducted into a church that allowed people to lead with no consequences to sin, error, or accountability. I was a faithful member to the church of humanity. It sounds strange when announced like that, but are you a member?

This church stands with the statement of faith that we are only human. This excuses the accountability that comes with Christian living and leadership within the Body of CHRIST. I am not denying the frailties that lie within each and every one of us, but when did it become okay to answer sin with excuses that tout a don't-judge-me message? Where are the screams of a brokenness that acknowledge, "I was wrong and I want to be restored"? Where is the restored leadership that becomes transparent with a determination that will bear all so that the trap and proclivities that claim hundreds and even thousands at their sin have a voice crying in the wilderness that there is a better way?

Deception is strong and strategic to the church hurt festering in the Body of CHRIST. Often, the fact is, no one wants to deal with the reality of our conditions, and because of the implications of truth, they choose to rest in the comfort of being deceived.

If I claim I don't see it, then what responsibility do I have to deal with it? According to the Macmillan Dictionary, deception is defined as the act of deceiving or being deceived. Deception is a dual poison. It cannot be given without being received. Deception is a tool that is often implemented by the devil with the ultimate purpose to stop the conversion and healing of a person. The enemy understands that if he can lock us up in lies, we will never be set free. **John 8:32 (KJV)** states, *"And you shall know the Truth and the Truth will set you free."*

In intercession for the Body of CHRIST, GOD

challenged me to pray against deception. This question of deception plagued me and caused me to seek GOD for greater understanding. The question that challenged me was how one gets entangled in deception. I use the word, "entangled," because deception is like a web that locks us into a position and stops our spiritual momentum.

As I was looking outward to find my answers, an inner tug told me that my search need not go too far. During a session in prayer, GOD showed me a vision of a wash bucket with spiders floating on the top. I immediately understood the revelation but simultaneously assumed that this was for someone else. I boasted to my mom that GOD was washing someone of deception. I did so with the mention of someone else's name and she then challenged me with the question, "Could it be you that GOD is washing of deception?"

Immediate defense entered. "Not me!" I thought, "I am righteous. I fast and pray. I seek GOD continually." My defense was an alarm that help was needed.

I earnestly sought GOD to understand what He was saying. On first approach to this subject, I could readily see how other mighty men and women of GOD were deceived by looking at them. Their many actions and continuing erroneous stand told me that we could not be reading and understanding the same Scriptures. I could easily point fingers and stand on my righteous soap box, yell until the cows came home, and rant about the deceit and treachery that I witnessed at the hands of those who claimed titles of the most spiritual elite. Yet it was my own heart that had grown fat.

Rantings Of A Crazy Woman

Book Excerpt

WELCOME TO MY WORLD

Welcome to my world - one that is consistently crazy! During the compilation of these stories, I was in an interesting place. I was going to church with a smile on my face but coming home thinking that there has got to be more than this. Don't get me wrong. My ministry was taking off, but it still felt like a walk that should have been a run. People looking on the outside thought that my life was peaches and cream, which is fine for some, but GOD promised me strawberry shortcake. I was very aware that this is not it! Through that time, I started getting distracted.

This distraction was deadly. It consumed my focus and retarded my stride. It could have been catastrophic if left unchecked. It was the dark shadow that clouded my sunny days, constantly lurking around, demanding my attention.

This distraction was not a man. My distraction was called lack spiritual lack, emotional lack, physical lack, financial lack, and relational lack. I allowed it to announce itself on every level. As I looked at the vision that I was to run and how ill equipped I was, I began to panic. My panic led to frustration and then inner turmoil. I was looking at the picture of my destiny, trying to decipher the many colors. The colors started bleeding and blending to the point I did not know where one color stopped and another began. It was tiring.

No one knew. Being saved for a considerable amount of time allows for some very skilled performances. We know what to say and how to act. I had it down pat. I can minister to you and you never know that I am hurting. I found it hard to trust others to handle my pain, so I masked it beyond excellent service. Mind you, the service isn't fake; it is genuine, but hollow.

I found it easy to believe the LORD for others. For others, I can tear down walls and leap over troops. I will fight for them. But very seldom did I find it easy to fight for me. I would put my needs on the back burner until I smelled smoke. What was in the pot to serve a hungry people became inedible. Reverently afraid of making someone sick because of ill prepared food, I stopped cooking my own food and just assisted others with their meal.

It is easy to hide behind the crowd. But when GOD is calling one to lead, the need for obedience becomes crucial because the reality is, someone is waiting for your obedience.

Thoughts of a Virgin

IDELLA LISELLE

EXPLICIT ON PURPOSE

Thoughts of A Virgin Book Excerpt

THE CHASTITY BELT FROM HELL

I was 10 years old when they pushed a boy on top of me and told us to "do it." My panic caused me to scream out, "no I don't want to have sex now, I want to be a virgin until I am 11,12, 13, 14, 15, 16, …" The counting stopped when they pulled the other young boy off me.

The whole group of children were older than me and ranged in ages from 12-15. I was the youngest. I had skipped two grades, so my peers were typically older than me. They laughed hysterically at the episode. For them, I am sure they considered it nothing serious. Though we were both fully clothed, the fear I felt that day left me exposed, vulnerable, and helpless. Feeling the weight of him on me caused my heart to race as my pushing was inadequate to get him off. Images of rape scenes from afternoon specials were being played in my thoughts.

As I stood up, I laughed it off in my typical fashion, not wanting to bring attention to myself. At that age, I wasn't connected enough with my emotions to recognize the effect of that moment or to stand up for myself.

My childhood was surrounded with an abnormal

amount of sexual awareness and activity. Our after-school activities were consumed with girls and boys "hunching." This is where the children simulated sex with their clothes on. Though as a child, I never participated, I was still exposed to it.

At a young age, I recall my mother explaining sex to me in a very scientific manner. My mother was very open about sex and procreation. She was open to our questions. Which made me the sex awareness spokesman bringing correction to youthful fallacies at our Christian school.

Often the other girls would try to make me feel bad because I was not sexually active like them. These 10 and 11year old girls were bragging about having sex. Understanding that hunching wasn't sex, I recall using my knowledge to burst their bubbles.

There was time, a girl said she had sex with her boyfriend, and I asked her very bluntly if he inserted his penis into her vagina. The look on her face was priceless. She turned up her lips and screeched, "oooh noo." My response of victory wasn't withheld but released immediately with a satisfied glee, "well you are a virgin just like me., how you like those apples?".

I was raised by a Christian mom who lived CHRIST before us in such faithfulness in integrity. She reinforced our need to represent well. She raised us to be leaders, and being a leader meant being mindful of choices and opportunities. She reminded us that every time we walked out the doors, we should represent 3 people with excellence. GOD, her as a mother and my race. These responsibilities at times created a need for perfection. It wasn't because my mother ever said that was what she expected but I personally never wanted to disappoint her.

I therefore, at times struggled to perform because I didn't want to let anyone down. I created unrealistic expectations even for myself and put unbearable standards on myself. I was known as the church girl. Yet I had some bad girl tendencies. That responsibility of being the church girl worked well for me until it didn't.

A Praying Mother
Book Excerpt

My mother taught us that HOLY SPIRIT could tell us things we didn't know. We were not able to confess we couldn't do something. She imposed Philippians 4:13 as an active place of accountability.

Her prayer life had undeniable evidence. When I was a missionary in Mexico at the age of 17, I got a message to call my mother. As I stood outside at the public payphone, I heard my mother's voice. She asked, "What's going on? We have been praying for you." I shared that I was frustrated because I couldn't communicate with people effectively. I was limited to charades to get my point across. I said I was ready to come back because I could witness in English in the states. She listened intently and then asked me this question. "Do you think GOD can give you the "gift" of speaking Spanish? I responded with an emphatic, "yes, GOD can do anything." She then said, let's pray.

She prayed that GOD would give me the gift of speaking Spanish and that speaking Spanish would be as easy as speaking English and that my mind would be able to think in Spanish, she continued on for another minute or two, and we closed it out with an amen. My spirit was encouraged, and two weeks later, I was translating. The girl who couldn't roll her r's had dreams in Spanish. The gift at that time was so profound that when I spoke, it was thought that I too was from a Spanish speaking country.

I have so many stories of supernatural evidence from my mother's prayers. Growing up, there was a prayer we prayed daily. I remember as my mother wrote it out, it seemed it was so long. I remember it taking an hour at times to pray. She continued adding to that prayer as GOD provided more insight and revelation, the prayer got longer. My mother would pray for us every day. I recall near her passing, she told us that she would no longer be covering us daily like that anymore it was now our responsibility to cover ourselves.

I have included that prayer with some new HOLY SPIRIT inspired additions. I pray that this prayer positions you and your children to experience a prayer life of power, signs, and wonders.

"Now set your heart and your soul to seek the LORD your God; arise, therefore, and build the sanctuary of the LORD God, so that you may bring the ark of the covenant of the LORD
and the holy vessels of God into the house that is to be built for the name of the LORD."
1 Chronicles 22:19

    I love this Scripture. It sets what I consider the framework for prayer. This illustrates the importance of the prep work necessary to seek the Lord
and build an atmosphere that provokes the presence of GOD and calls forth the tools required for GOD's purpose to be fulfilled in the earth.
    These are the steps I encourage for more effectiveness prayer.

\\YOUR NAME BELONGS HERE //www.PUBLISHHER.org

THE DIARY OF A BAD GIRL

KINGDOM STYLE
VOLUME ONE

IDELLA LISELLE

FROM DIARY OF A BAD GIRL
BOOK EXCERPT

BAD ON PURPOSE

But as for you, you meant evil against me; but GOD meant it for good, in order to bring it about as it is this day, to save many people alive.   Genesis 50:20

Have you ever felt like life had it in for you? I mean, even from birth, you felt like the odds were always stacked against you. These thoughts almost breed a sense of helplessness. The next thing we know is that we are living a life braced for impact, always expecting the other shoe to drop. To add salt to injury, a lack of a healthy foundation in early childhood allows for endless questioning of self- worth, value, and purpose. Those on the outside would think that it was a setup for failure, but through more discerning eyes, one can see a masterful plan set in play, favored to have some interesting challenges in my life. At a young age, I knew there was something different about me. My dreams weren't the typical child's dreams.

While other children were dreaming of rainbows and lollipops, I was having dreams of fighting witches and warlocks. I was dreaming of saving drowning people or saving children, men, and women from buildings on the verge of collapsing.

I remember sharing some of those dreams in gory detail with my mother and her encouraging me that I had power even in my dreams. She told me to use the name of JESUS and that I was able to do anything in my dreams. That piece of information was the game changer. No longer was I being tormented in my dreams. The fear was gone. Now, no matter what tried to appear, I knew I was powerful. I would fly in my dreams and walk on water in my dreams. Even as a child, I knew that there were some places where I could be unstoppable.

As for my dream space, I had that down, but my waking moments still had their bout of issues. At an early age, I was introduced to perversion. I was first shown how to touch myself at 7 by another little girl at daycare. Then I saw my first pornographic magazine at the age of 9 with my brother and some neighborhood boys. At the age of 11, I was molested by a female family friend who had probably also been molested. The trap was set.

Order Your Copies Today
www.idellaliselle.com

WIFE MATERIAL

www.ingramcontent.com/pod-product-compliance
Lightning Source LLC
Chambersburg PA
CBHW062209080426
42734CB00010B/1849